BIANCA CAPPELLO.

A TRAGEDY.

BIANCA CAPPELLO

A TRAGEDY

BY

ELIZABETH C. KINNEY

NEW YORK
PUBLISHED BY HURD AND HOUGHTON
1873

RIVERSIDE, CAMBRIDGE:
STEREOTYPED AND PRINTED BY
H. O. HOUGHTON AND COMPANY.

SOME OF THE HISTORICAL AUTHORITIES FOR THE FACTS OF THE DRAMA.

Napier's *Florentine History.*

Florence et ses Vicissitudes. By Monsieur Delécluse.

L' Osservatore Fiorentino.

Memorie di Bianca Cappello. By Stefano Ticozzi, etc., etc.

PERSONS OF THE DRAMA.

FRANCESCO, *Prince Regent, afterwards Grand Duke of Florence, and son of Cosimo de Medici.*
FERDINANDO, *Cardinal de Medici, brother of Francesco.*
SERGUIDI, *minister, and confidant of the Prince Regent.*
FRA FORTUNATO, *a monk, confidant of Ferdinando.*
BARTOLOMEO CAPPELLO, *a Venetian nobleman, and father of Bianca.*
PATRIARCH D'AQUILEA, *his brother.*
ROBERTO RICCI, *a noble Florentine.*
MANDRAGONI, *maêstro of the ducal palace.*
BUONAVENTURI, *humble citizen of Florence.*
PIETRO, *his son.*
GIOVANNI, *servant of the Cardinal.*
JEANNE, *Archduchess of Austria, wife of Francesco.*
BIANCA CAPPELLO, *wife of Pietro.*
MADAME MANDRAGONI, *wife of the maêstro.*
COSTANZA, *wife of Buonaventuri, and mother of Pietro.*
ANNE, *Austrian maid of the Archduchess.*
Citizens, servants, etc.

SCENE: *at Venice, Florence and its environs.*
TIME: *latter part of the sixteenth century.*

Scene I. — *Venice.*

Grand Canal by moonlight. Bartolomeo Cappello *and* Patriarch d'Aquilea *issue hastily from a palace, conversing in an excited manner.*

AQUILEA.

Peace! peace, my lord! This is a fruitless rage;
Husband thy forces for judicial acts.

CAPPELLO.

Talk not of peace — war only is the word!
Already civil war is in my heart —
Pride wrestles there with pride: that proud intent,
To wed my only daughter with a prince,
Hath driven her from me with a beggar's son,
And thus the strife within which makes me mad.

AQUILEA.

What! hast no thought of vengeance? now, by Heaven!
I thought our blood was nobler than the asp's,
Which turns to pierce itself with that same sting
Whose venom might have worked its own escape!
I am for vengeance! not ignoble war:

Bianca is my niece, and if thou, brother,
Being thyself her sire, wilt nothing do,
But sting thy soul to frenzy, then — leave me!
I need no aid save what these veins can give,
Each purple drop is loyal to my will.
Adieu! who acts, but loses force in words.

[*Going.*

CAPPELLO.

[*Following.*

Stay! I will go with thee; I see thy bile
Flows more in keeping with thy blood, than mine.

[*They enter together a gondola in waiting, and depart.*

SCENE II. — *Florence.*

Mean apartment in the house of BUONAVENTURI. COSTANZA *engaged in arranging the room.*

COSTANZA.

My wits must work to do the best I can,
And at the best, this is no fitting place
To lodge a high-born, gentle lady in.
How could Pietro have forgot my words,
That he who reaches higher than his height
Loses all foothold, bringing to the ground,
In his own fall, a lordly pride whose weight
Must crush his humble fortunes underneath.

Enter BUONAVENTURI.

BUONAVENTURI.

Ah, wife, and you are ready for them! well,
Put the best face on 't; by this time, perchance,
The strange young lady is as pale and sick
Of her own will, as the green sailor grows
Of sea-room, when the waves begin to swell.

COSTANZA.

Oh, yes; and she 's but our poor daughter now;
So let us open to her parent-hearts.

The harbor of our love is small and mean;
But now, let loose from any other hold,
Her heart may gladly cast its anchor here.

BUONAVENTURI.

Hark! on the stair I hear approaching steps;
Haste, wife, adjust thy cap and brow, to suit
An honest greeting, and a mother's smile.

Enter Pietro *and* Bianca: *the parents encounter and embrace them.*

BUONAVENTURI.

[*To* Bianca.

As warm a welcome as warm hearts can give!
No worthier will our humble home afford,
But, what it lacks in fitting ornament,
Thy gentleness and beauty will supply.

COSTANZA.

[*To* Bianca.

Great honor dost thou to our meaner house
To wed thee with Pietro; but, fair dame,
If he shall prove to thee a husband true,
As unto us he ever was a son,
Thou hast not stooped from thy high rank for naught.

BIANCA.

Thanks to ye, for the shelter and the love
Proffered to me, a stranger, for his sake,
To you as son, to me as husband dear!

Heaven make me worthy of your honest hearts;
And may you find that you 've not lost a son,
But gained a daughter in my father's loss.

[*Weeps;* COSTANZA *embraces her.*

PIETRO.

[*To his parents.*

And you shall prize in her no common gain;
Believe me, honored parents, if I dared
To reach above me, 'gainst your staid advice,
'Twas for a jewel worthy any risk.

BIANCA.

[*To* PIETRO, *assuming a gay smile.*

Your jewel will be brighter in the sun;
Too dull it looks now to confirm that boast.

[*To* COSTANZA.

With your kind leave I will at once retire:
Sleep should be sweet again beneath the roof
Where broods parental love with careful wing.

BUONAVENTURI.

[*Taking* BIANCA *by the hand.*

First go with us and join our frugal board;
Dreams are but nourishment for empty heads, —
The empty stomach needs more solid food.

[*Exeunt.*

Scene III. — *The Same.*

A small chamber, the bed hidden by a curtain: enter Costanza, *with a light in her hand, followed by* Bianca.

COSTANZA.

It is a simple chamber, but thine own:
Make thee at home then here as best thou canst.

BIANCA.

All must be well that thoughtful love prepares;
Thanks for thy kindness, and to thee good night!

COSTANZA.

[*Putting down the light, and approaching to aid her.*

First, let me help thee, or thou 'lt miss thy nurse;
I never had a daughter, but, methinks,
A woman cannot be too old to learn
The nicer cares which suit not lusty boys,
And care makes up the sum of mother's bliss.

BIANCA.

For lack of girls then, thou of me must learn
That 't is the daughter should the mother aid;
And this rough journey hath so seasoned me,

That I shall never shrink to useless stuff,
But serve thee in some manner — not thou me:
So now, good mother, fare thee well till morn.

[*Kissing her.*

COSTANZA.

[*Going.*

And gentle be thy dreamings, as thy ways!
Good night — God bless thee!

BIANCA.

Ay, and thee, kind heart!

[*Exit* COSTANZA.

Would that I were as worthy to be blest!

[*Looks about her.*

But whither have I come — is this my home?
Where are the dear familiar things, but late
Unheeded for their very commonness?
Those every-day-used, unfelt luxuries?
Oh! each, the smallest, here would grow in size
To something that might break the staring void;
Had I but my poor nurse beside me now,
Methinks this desert want would wear a smile, —
No place is sterile where lives sympathy;
But, like a snake, I slid from her embrace,
Leaving my fault to sting her innocence.

[*Listens.*

Hark, 't is Pietro's step! I must to bed.

[*Disappears behind the curtain.*

SCENE IV. — *The Same.*

Morning. Mean apartment as in Scene II. BIANCA *alone, regarding herself in a small mirror.*

BIANCA.

Well, I slept soundly as a wearied child;
Pietro's jewel looks in sooth more bright
In this clear sun, than dimmed, as late, by tears.

Enter PIETRO *with open letters in his hand.*

PIETRO.

My own Bianca! here 's sad news for us —
But, turn not pale — Oh, I am all too rash!

BIANCA.

[*Rising excitedly.*

Regard not me — come, quick, discharge thy load!
Suspense is a dull saw, that tortures slowly;
Harsh truth, at worst, the sharpened axe's blade,
Which does its execution at a blow.

PIETRO.

Well, if thou wilt the worst — these letters say
That thy stern uncle hath imprisoned mine,
In our default; and that thy father's rage
Is by the patriarch so goaded on,

That it will end in our divorce — by Death!
Their emissaries now are on our track,
And these are sworn — the oath made sure by gold —
To bring their swords back reeking in my blood;
But I have told thee not to blanch thy cheeks;
I would consult thee of a plan proposed,
Which may secure us strength to match our need.

BIANCA.

And what think'st thou our simple wits could work,
Against such force by haughty vengeance armed?
Oh! if they touch a hair of thy dear head,
The daughter's blood shall pay the father's wrath.

PIETRO.

But it shall never have so dear a price:
I am advised to ask the Prince's aid.
Already knows he of our misadventures,
And predisposed is now to succor us.
'T is known that Cosimo, weary of state rule,
Hath given his son the governmental reins.
Serguidi is Francesco's minister,
And friendly to my other kinsman, too,
(The monk who entertained us by the way,)
And knows through him my uncle's unjust fate;
Unto Serguidi then I will betake me,
And he shall plead our cause before the Prince,
Who is himself of such a kindly nature
That, sure am I, he 'll not deny the suit:
So in the end we may defeat ill-luck.

BIANCA.

Yes, go; and promptness will secure prompt aid;
Something premonishes my heart, as thine,
That we shall yet prevail o'er these proud foes;
The smallest chance of such a victory
Is worth the largest effort.

PIETRO.

Then adieu!
Let hope call back the sunshine to thy brow.
I see its dawn now in that rosy tint,
And thus salute joy's fair returning day.
[*Kisses her forehead and departs.*

BIANCA. [*Alone.*

Love, thou art sweet! yet there 's a sweeter joy,
Methinks, in conquering imperious foes:
Oh! I could almost sell the wealth I own
In that true heart, for which all else I sold,
To drink the satisfying cup of triumph,
Filled to the brim, before my enemies!
Yet, I know goodness is the strongest arm
With which to shame them, or to conquer them.
[*Pauses a moment.*
I should content me with this lowly lot,
Punish with my own happiness my foes;
Or, through majestic pardon awe them down.
I will go seek the honest pair; with them
My heart grew meek, my nature softer seemed:
Evil comes nearest when we are alone. [*Exit.*

SCENE V. — *The Same.*

Cabinet in the royal palace. Enter the PRINCE REGENT *and* SERGUIDI.

PRINCE.

[*Sitting down.*

Now tell me what is truth in this romance;
Give me a history of simple facts:
For, to believe these many-tongued reports,
Would be one day to bless propitious Luck
For having brought a human angel here;
Another day to curse perfidious Fate
For a sly devil in an angel's form.

SERGUIDI.

Your Highness now shall have th' ungarnished tale,
With the true portrait of the heroine:
Bianca is of that right noble blood
Cappello — house of proud Venetian boast!
Her mother, of no less illustrious stock,
Yielded life up in giving life to her;
And in her tender years, her father took
A stately wife whose heart matched not her size, —
Having but room to take her own child in,
And not a whit of love to spare from him

For wasting on the offspring of another;
Nay, did forbid his larger, richer heart,
To coin for her a sister's precious name.
In brief, the sum of her maternal care
Was seeking, piously, a mother true
For the fair orphan in the nursing Church.

PRINCE.

Not the first time the Church a pretext was,
To serve a selfish end.

SERGUIDI.

A woman's art —
True handmaid to her will — is seldom foiled;
The father, in the husband's yoke subdued,
Yielded consent, and gave his daughter up.
Meantime, as luck would have it, good or ill,
Bianca's eyes encountered other eyes,
And in that meeting of live passion's sparks
A fire was kindled reason might not quench;
Love burnt out pride; and then stored all its wealth
In this bold Florentine, by chance at Venice,
Who matched her only in his daring flame.

PRINCE.

The same old tale, new told!

SERGUIDI.

They met by stealth:
Now at, then going to, the holy mass;

And last at midnight, through false keys supplied
By love's necessity inventive grown —
To them the golden keys of Paradise.
But, as of old, the serpent lurked near by,
And so it fell their Paradise was lost.

PRINCE.

The girl 's a heroine!

SERGUIDI.

She knew her chance —
Her only chance of love — would soon be bound
By the stern convent's walls, and fain would taste
One draught of sweet, before her lips were sealed
Against warm kisses by cold vestal vows.
But, so it happened, an old prince of wealth
Asked for her hand, and in that asking spoiled
The father's good intent to wed his child
To Christ, and gain for her Heaven's heritage.

PRINCE.

Ah, gold and titles often buy the sum
Of good intentions!

SERGUIDI.

So, the haughty sire —
In pride o'ergrown before 't was ripe — would give
A foretaste of ambition's fruit to her.
She found it sour, the golden apple spurned,

And, proving sweeter love's forbidden fruit,
Resolved to venture everything for this;
So, with a stranger fled in darkest night,
Without acquainting even her trusty nurse.

PRINCE.

If equal be her beauty to her courage,
Too rich such prize for a plebeian's hand!

SERGUIDI.

Through perils on the land and on the sea,
They hither came, and now, in wedlock joined,
Are meanly lodged beneath the humble roof
Of the youth's father, honest Buon'venturi.

PRINCE.

But wherefore, and in what, ask they our aid?

SERGUIDI.

The sequel of my tale is yet to tell:
All Venice was in uproar at their flight;
But love, that sharpens even the dullest wit,
Evaded every search; while anger, foiled,
Vented its spleen upon the innocent.
Among its other wrongs, it hath imprisoned
Pietro's uncle, in his nephew's stead,
Swearing to take no other bail for him
Than the girl's presence, or her husband's life —
Threatened each moment, Prince, with violence.

The facts are these: your Highness now will say
What shall be done.

PRINCE.

Yes; but not all is told:
Thou, in the story, hast forgot to give
The heroine's portrait.

SERGUIDI.

Hard were this to give:
'T were better that your Highness saw the face,
Than that I painted it.

PRINCE.

Then she 's not fair:
For beauty gives man's tongue such vivid hues,
That, as it speaks, upon the listener's mind
Is painted every grace.

SERGUIDI.

And beauty too,
Of certain force, strikes dumb; and such is hers:
If I should say she was so short, so tall,
Had such and such decided traits, and such
Known graces as pronounce all others fair,
I should be just as far from painting her
As reason would be from portraying love.
Love ne'er was known except when it was felt;
Nor beauty of such kind e'er painted, save
By its own self upon the heart.

PRINCE.

Enough!
To-morrow bid Bianca and her spouse
To private audience here.

[*Rising.*

SERGUIDI.

It shall be done.

[*Exit* PRINCE.

The bait has taken; now my end is sure:
His princely appetite, thus keenly whetted,
Will do the rest. O man! thy boasted force,
Backed even by the puissance of a throne,
Is weaker than weak woman's weakest charm,
When armed to conquer by her sovereign will.

[*Exit.*

SCENE VI. — *The Same.*

A lonely street, in sight of a church. Enter rapidly COSTANZA *and* BIANCA, *on their way to vespers.*

COSTANZA.

Stop here a moment, child, and take new breath;
The church is close at hand, and we are safe
Now in its sacrèd shadow; rest thy fears.
'T is right we go to prayer, for I believe
That prayers of honest wives and mothers have
A private entrance to the throne of Heaven,
Which for their special wants stands ever open.
[*The bell sounds.*

BIANCA.

Hark, there's the bell! come, mother, let us on:
I tremble, and yet know not why, to pause,
As some poor hare with hounds upon her track.

COSTANZA.

[*Leading her on.*

Keep closer to me, then, and we'll proceed;
But slower, child, there is no need of haste.

[*Noise behind arrests their steps. Enter armed Brigands dragging* PIETRO, *while* BUONAVENTURI *follows, expostulating with them.*

1ST BRIGAND.

Stand back, old man!

BUONAVENTURI.

Let go my son, my son!

BIANCA.

[*Running to her husband.*

Oh, it is he!

[*To* 1ST BRIGAND.

It is my husband, man,
Release him from these ruffians!

COSTANZA.

Mercy, pray!

1ST BRIGAND.

Peace, women! he 's our prisoner, and must go.

[BIANCA *clings to* PIETRO. 1ST BRIGAND *tries to force her away.*

BIANCA.

Unhand me, brigand!

[*To* BUONAVENTURI.

Go thou, call for help!

[*A Brigand seizes* BUONAVENTURI, *who is going.*

1ST BRIGAND.

Out on ye all! Revenge must have its way:
We come from Venice, and must take this rogue,

[*Pointing to* PIETRO.

Dead or alive, back there.

PIETRO.

[*To* BIANCA.

'T is vain, love, vain —
Take off thy dear hands — we must part; adieu!

BIANCA.

Never! where'er they take thee, I will go;
Howe'er they serve thee, I will share thy fate.

[1ST BRIGAND *goes to force her away, when the* PRINCE REGENT *enters with* SERGUIDI, *Guards following them.*

SERGUIDI.

[*To the* PRINCE.

Heavens, 't is Bianca!

PRINCE.

Hold, assassins! hold!

[*To his Guards.*

Secure these murderers, and lead them off!

[*Guards seize the ruffians.*

1ST BRIGAND.

In this lone hour and street our prey seemed sure;
We 've lost it, our reward, and freedom too.

[*Exeunt Guards with Brigands.*

BIANCA.

[*Throwing herself at the* PRINCE'S *feet.*

O Prince! as mercy's angel have you come:
Heaven bless your Highness!

PRINCE.

[*Raising her up.*

Yes; in blessing thee!

PIETRO.

[*Kneeling.*

The life my Prince has saved, he hence will use:
This heart was ever loyal, but now owes
Its blood, were each drop doubled, to its sovereign.

PRINCE.

We shall accept thy services, and find
Some post of safety for thee; fear thou not!

BUONAVENTURI.

[*Approaching with his wife, and inclining.*

Gray hairs can only render thanks in blessings:
Saving our son, Prince, you prolong our days,
And while they last, each one anew shall bless you.

PRINCE.

A prince's subjects all are sons to him:
Go ye in peace! — hence I will guard my own,
And thus protect one dearer still to you.

[*To* Bianca, *speaking low.*

To aid your cause, I needs must learn your tale,
And those lips best will tell it: come to-morrow,
At midday, with Pietro, to the palace:
Till then, adieu! your foes are in safe keeping.

COSTANZA.

[*Taking* BIANCA'S *hand and speaking to her husband and son.*

Come you to church now, with us, and give thanks.

[*Exeunt, bowing reverently to the* PRINCE.

PRINCE.

[*Looking after them.*

Is that a creature of this lower sphere?
The first-born smile of Heaven was not more fair!
How her voice, love-toned as soft summer airs,
Played magic on this heart's ecstatic strings!
And she seemed shapen by its harmony —
Herself as music's very soul embodied,
So I became all eyes, all ears at once.

[*Various persons cross the stage slowly, regarding the* PRINCE.

SERGUIDI.

The street, Prince, will become all eyes, all ears,
If we still tarry here.

PRINCE.

Yes — to the palace.

[*Exeunt.*

ACT II.

Scene I. — *The Same.*

Audience-chamber in the palace. The Prince Regent *seated,* Serguidi *standing by him. Enter an Usher.*

PRINCE.

Conduct them hither without further form.

Usher leads in Bianca *and* Pietro, *and retires.* Francesco *rises and takes* Bianca's *hand to seat her by his side, but she courtesies and continues standing, while he reseats himself.*

[*To* Bianca.

Proceed to tell thy tale; have no reserve.

BIANCA.

'T is long to suffer, but 't is brief to tell:
Your Highness knows I am the only daughter
Of a patrician, senator of Venice.
Grief's winter hath invaded my life's spring,
Hath nipped the budding joys of infancy,
Robbed of its sunshine a fond mother's smile.
My noble father loved me, but his love
Was more in praises than caresses shown;
Nor could his lofty wife e'er stoop so low
As to dry childhood's simple tears from one
Who needs must weep that she was motherless.

The first to love me was my tender nurse,
Whose absence I had ne'er to mourn till now;
But she, to soften more my rigid lot,
Trained me with such an over-fond indulgence,
That my heart grew but sicklier for her care,
Craving some aliment, 'twixt bitter scorn
And sweetest fondness, which my father's heart,
So proudly kind, could never quite supply.
When I met him who is my husband now,
That twin-born sympathy awoke to life
Which feeds the heart, while on the heart it feeds;
So strong I grew on this true nourishment,
That, having feasted, I could hence have lived
Upon its memory in a convent's cell;
But, when my father bade me wed another,
Repugnance pushed with force against his will,
While love's indissoluble cords still drew
My fortunes with my heart to its true lord.
Pardon! your Highness knows the rest.

PRINCE.

Say on!
To pour thy heart will lighten it, at least.

BIANCA.

Such bounty, Prince, as deigns to listen thus,
Needs not the urging of weak words: yet these
Would fain the guard of royal favor ask,
To invest the life in which my own is bound.

[*Throws herself weeping before the* PRINCE; PIETRO *kneels behind her.*

Oh, succor him who is my all on earth!

PRINCE.

[*Raising her up.*

Rise; weep no more! Your dangers now are past.

[*Puts a ring on her finger.*

This be the seal of our protection hence.
We have sent back to Venice, under guard,
The bold invaders of your peace and lives;
With such remonstrance as will hence secure
Your persons and your rights from violence.
Dwell then at ease in mind, and look for change
That shall procure you ease of circumstance.
Adieu, until ye hear from us again.

[*Exeunt* BIANCA *and* PIETRO *joyfully, accompanied by* SERGUIDI.

Did I e'er look on beauty — ever feel
What woman's charm was, till I saw that face?
Serguidi 's right; no tongue could fitly paint her,
Unless it were the tongue of Love itself;
No pencil, save it stole ethereal colors.
Her spiritual charm — 't is like the sky,
That, while the painter dips his brush to catch it,
Changes its phase, and looks him to despair.

Reënter SERGUIDI.

How now, Serguidi, has she gone? what said she?
How looked she? did she smile on going hence?

If so, haste, tell it! ere I strike thee dumb
For having seen a smile which I saw not:
Come! why so slow of speech?

SERGUIDI.

Your pardon, Prince!
I had no place to put a word till now;
She has gone hence, and I've brought back her smiles,
To grace the thanks she bade me here to lay,
Beside her husband's, at her Prince's feet.

PRINCE.

Name not her base-born spouse in naming her!

SERGUIDI.

Your Highness sees now what I could not paint.
Perchance the fault was in too coarse a tongue;
Yet royal lips may have the finer touch
Befitting royal beauty, and can paint her.

PRINCE.

She is not to be painted, trait by trait,
As one paints easily mere dainty flesh.

SERGUIDI.

Then hers are something more than mortal charms?

PRINCE.

Out on thy bantering! had I now my throne,

The Church, which hath ignobly bound her once,
Should, through its Head, release her from this bond,
And she whom beauty crowns should share that
throne;
But thus we cannot use a father's crown.
By what means, then, to win her?

SERGUIDI.

Regal means,
Have stronger proved than legal, before now;
What princes have done, princes may do still.
The meanest love, it seems, hath royal might,
And love born royal should have power no less.

PRINCE.

The chance is worth the trial — we shall try;
Thou hast a ready faculty to see,
And wit to serve it.

SERGUIDI.

From your Highness' wish
Cometh the wit, as doth the will to serve;
I now bethink me —

PRINCE.

Speak! what wouldst thou say?

SERGUIDI.

That Mandragoni's wife should first be gained;
And leave a woman, then, to spy out for us

The promised land, if Love would have possession;
Meantime the price —

PRINCE.

No price, save love, will buy
What befits love.

SERGUIDI.

But, what 's sold for love
Must first re-purchased be with baser coin,
Ere it can sell itself for love again;
So, while the wiles of the maëstro's wife
Work with Bianca, buy her through her spouse;
My wits for 't! his is vanity so light
That, once blown up, 't will give to air his love;
While gold will build him castles in the air,
And stars of honor dazzle him to blindness.

PRINCE.

You 're right, Serguidi; gain him, and we 'll blind
him!
But, of Bianca?

SERGUIDI.

There 's no fear of her:
Women love strongest where ambition draws.
Your Highness thinks it but a paradox,
Yet Love 's the greatest of all egotists,
And he loves most, who most his own self loves;
Sometimes 't is bliss of loving that Love loves,

And for the joy of being loved again.
Self-sacrificing love is but a name
For friendship superfine, and does in truth,
Self-sacrificing, sacrifice to self,
To gain the soul's applause and praise of Heaven.

PRINCE.

And in what better is the courtier's love?

SERGUIDI.

In naught, your Highness; though he who loves self,
Best loves and serves his sovereign.

PRINCE.

Sophistry!
Thou hast the head, Serguidi, for our plans:
Serve best thyself, then, in best serving them.

[*Exit.*

SERGUIDI.

Ay, that I will! and grow so in his need,
That all the odds between us his crown makes
Shall be, that he will wear it, and I use it.

[*Exit.*

SCENE II. — *The Same.*

A gallery in the palace. FRANCESCO *seen walking thoughtfully alone. Enter, unseen by him, the* CARDINAL FERDINANDO.

PRINCE.

I said that none could paint her, trait by trait;
Yet every charm seems of itself the painter,
And on my heart has left its special image!

[CARDINAL *comes forward;* PRINCE *starts on seeing him.*

Well, brother?

CARDINAL.

You 're preoccupied I see.
Raving as wont, of some new beauty, Prince?

PRINCE.

Ha! did thought speak so loud?

CARDINAL.

I heard alone;
'T was lucky — others might perchance have heard;
Be cautious when you thus love's secrets tell.

PRINCE.

What said I, then?

CARDINAL.

What I cared not to hear;
Something, I think, which nearer touches you
Than your betrothal.

PRINCE.

[*Frowning.*

Brother, change your theme;
All other subjects now would better please.

CARDINAL.

And one, it seems, above all others; Prince,
Would you repeat what I just heard you say?

PRINCE.

First tell me what that was.

CARDINAL.

What could it be,
Save woman's charms — best theme for reverie!
Some new divinity your heart enshrines,
And hides her image from the envious day.

PRINCE.

At least you can divine —

CARDINAL.

What words declare!

PRINCE.

Well, you shall share the secret of my thoughts.

I 've seen a woman in whose single face
All heavenly and all human charms unite.

CARDINAL.

And you said every charm itself did paint
Upon your heart; pray draw the veil aside;
Let me at least behold that portrait, Prince.

PRINCE.

It lies too deep even for a brother's eye;
And words would fail to paint it yet again.

CARDINAL.

Let me put questions that will language teach
To shape those charms, and color them aright;
That which crowns all, the hair, it first should paint;
What texture this, — what color, black or fair?

PRINCE.

Ask the sun that, whose beams nest in its curls![1]
Her hair 's a wealth — it is "the golden fleece" —
A living brightness, shooting up such rays
As form an aureola round her head.

CARDINAL.

Then 't is a crown itself — she 'll not need yours;
And has she eyes to match it? what of these?

[1] The portraits of Bianca Cappello represent her style of beauty as more classical than Italian.

PRINCE.

Her eyes — I seem still looking in their depths! —
Are crystal wells, full ever to the brim,
That deepen thrice heaven's blue which they reflect;
To gaze in them, is each time to discern
Some star that never dazzled sight before.

CARDINAL.

I see that you have turned star-gazer, Prince,
And so, perchance, no eyes had for her skin.

PRINCE.

Her skin? 't is like a pure white rose's leaf,
Mirroring by wax-light the pink one above it;
Her temples, the transparence of her neck,
Mother of pearl, with turquoise veins inlaid.

CARDINAL.

Faith, you 're in love — you talk in poesy!
Has she a human form, and features such
As suit a mortal's taste?

PRINCE.

If he be king:
For Nature made a queenly soul the model
When, moulding into life such form and traits,
She curved her nostrils for the air of courts;
Pouted her proud lips for a royal kiss;
Between them strung the rarest pearls, for crowns;

And on her ivory shoulders set that neck
To grace, not be graced by, imperial gems.
Her hands were tapered to wear signet rings;
Her foot is light enough to tread on ermine.

CARDINAL.

[*With displeasure.*

You talk in earnest, brother; with your leave,
I will retire; Love needs no audience.

[FRANCESCO *bows assent; exit* CARDINAL.

PRINCE.

[*Alone.*

What is a crown worth, if it may not win
That which alone can crown our sovereign wish?
Shall monarchs reign to envy beggars' bliss,
Or, to possess it, through their royal right?
Could I by conquest gain earth's kingdoms all,
I should be powerless if I gained not her
Who hath already conquered me — who shall
In turn be conquered, if Love prove a god.

[*Exit.*

SCENE III. — *The Same.*

Chamber in BUONAVENTURI'S *house.* BIANCA *leaning thoughtfully on her hand; while* PIETRO *walks up and down the room with an air of gayety.*

PIETRO.

[*Stopping suddenly before his wife.*

What now, Bianca? as our fortunes clear,
Thou growest duller; not a right glad smile
I've seen these three days — since we saw the Prince.

BIANCA.

But thy face brightens up with fortune's smile,
So, what my own of pleasure's sunshine lacks,
Thine can supply, for thou wast ne'er so gay.

PIETRO.

And why keep brooding o'er a hapless past,
Or thankless present, when a glowing future
Laughs at them both, and beckons gayly on?

BIANCA.

[*Rising and approaching him lovingly.*

Ah, dearest! if our life's background be dark,
The heaven of love such brightness on it sheds,

That, from the present viewed, it seems all fair;
Those stolen kisses, snatched from midnight's heart,
Were sweeter to us than the breath of morn,
And turned the darkness ever into day.

PIETRO.

'T was but a taste, then, while the future menaced
To rob us even of that; now we may take
Our fill of love, with promise in advance
To sweeten it.

BIANCA.

[*Laying her hand gently on him.*

And art thou sure of that?
But what if with increase of fortune love
Decreases, will it richer fortune prove?

PIETRO.

Why ask such questions? does thy heart get cold,
As Fortune's warmer grows?

BIANCA.

And know'st thou not
That love, — which, destitute, could from itself
Create its warmth and food, and weave its bower,
As weaves her home the spider from within, —
When by capricious fortune once supplied
From outer life with cheating luxury,
Draws less and less from its warm inner source,
Till that itself dries up?

PIETRO.

A living source,
Dearest Bianca, is our pure, young love —
It cannot dry!

BIANCA.

Oh no, it never can!
To me 't would make an arid desert green;
Already hath it made this desert-home
All redolent of flowers —

PIETRO.

Say of one flower!
For all its sweetness is thy fond heart's breath,
And all its brightness what thy beauty gives.

[*Kisses her.*

BIANCA.

Oh, keep for thine own bosom then thy flower!
Be it a decoration, richer far
Than any gilded badge a crown could give.

PIETRO.

Stars would be well enough to wear outside;
But, fear not! I will keep my rose within.

BIANCA.

Nor sell it to a prince for gewgaws, love?

PIETRO.

Sell it! what talk you of, Bianca, pray!

Enter COSTANZA, *followed by* MANDRAGONI; BIANCA *starts back disconcertedly.*

MANDRAGONI.

A thousand pardons, Madam! but I come
At my wife's bidding; she the honor craves
Of your acquaintance, and has sent me here
To be your escort whither she awaits
Your gentle presence.

BIANCA.

Pray excuse me, sir!
You and your lady too much honor do
To our mean house and meaner company;
Another day, in more befitting garb,
I may accept your bounty.

MANDRAGONI.

Lady fair!
Beauty like yours is always well appareled.

COSTANZA.

[*Speaking in* BIANCA'S *ear.*

I fear some wile, my daughter; shun the snare.

BIANCA.

[*To* MANDRAGONI.

So late an hour befits not visits, sir;
To-morrow, if your lady will permit,
My husband shall conduct me.

MANDRAGONI.

Nay, to-night
He 'll do the same, and mine shall be the post
Of escort to you both.

PIETRO.

[*Exchanging looks with his wife.*

Too mean a post
For one whose place of honor is so high;
But we such bounty can no more refuse.

[*Exeunt* PIETRO *and* BIANCA *with* MANDRAGONI.

COSTANZA.

[*Alone.*

Alack! the bird obeys the fowler's snare;
Mother of God! keep her from being caught,
And our Pietro from a glittering shame!

[*Exit.*

Scene IV. — *The Same.*

Saloon in the part of the royal palace occupied by the Maëstro. Madame Mandragoni *and* Serguidi *seated together in conversation.*

SERGUIDI.

Sweeten thy bait well! thou as woman knowest
That every woman has her sweet tooth; some,
On honeyed compliments to beauty feed;
Some, on the extract, twice-refined, of praise
To higher qualities of mind or heart;
And some, on sweetest incense paid to them,
As to the sovereign holder of all charms.
But there are women who love, most of all,
The sweetness of obedience to their will;
To such, praise is ephemeral as light wine,
Exciting only for the passing moment;
Strong drink they need, which self-content can sweeten
To their taste better.

MADAME MANDRAGONI.

Shame, my lord! you talk
As if the inner characters of women
Were printed, like the letters in a book,
And you had read them all.

SERGUIDI.

No — not in books;
But I am something learned in women's eyes,
And have the key to certain signs of theirs,
Not easy to decipher.

MADAME MANDRAGONI.

You began
To talk of women, as if we were fish,
And you the dextrous angler who best knew
The way to catch us: so then, I am one,
And you are fishing!

SERGUIDI.

Pardon! when I speak
Of women there's one woman I except;
The proof that you are not among the fish,
Is that I make you angler 'mongst the men.

[*Aside.*

(How like a fish she catches at this bait!)

[*Aloud, and taking her hand.*

And who would not be caught by such an angler?

Enter MANDRAGONI *with* PIETRO *and* BIANCA; *exit* SERGUIDI *by another door, unseen by them.*

MANDRAGONI.

[*To his wife.*

Madam, this gentle lady meets your call,
And with her comes a happy husband too.

MADAME MANDRAGONI.

More welcomes, lady, than mere words can give,
And with them thanks for such prompt complaisance.

[*To* PIETRO.

Your presence, sir, but doubles our content.

BIANCA.

Not our mean costumes, nor ourselves, deserve
Such kind reception, Madam, — thanks are all
My presence here can bring, and these, if prized
By my own value, are too poor to pay.

MADAME MANDRAGONI.

Too rich, if thanks take worth from lips that speak,
And from the heart that yields them; nothing poor
Can come out of such lips.

[*Leads her to a seat.*

MANDRAGONI.

[*To* PIETRO.

Wilt favor me
With thy good company a moment, friend?
Ladies, anon we shall return again.

[*Exeunt* MANDRAGONI *and* PIETRO.

MADAME MANDRAGONI.

[*Seating herself by* BIANCA.

Our generous prince, sweet lady, takes thy cause
As much to heart as if it were the state's;
And well he may; for who could look on thee,

And not be touched that evil fortune touches
So at the root of beauty?

BIANCA.

Beauty, Madam,
A frail plant is at best, and soon uprooted
If its root strikes no deeper than the skin.

MADAME MANDRAGONI.

The blossom's form bespeaks the plant's true worth;
Here beauty is deep-rooted in the heart:
The Prince knows this — sees all misfortune crushes,
And would uplift it.

BIANCA.

By his Highness' grace,
I hope to lift myself up from the dust,
And teach such as would crush me that true power
Is not in the inflicting of misfortune,
But in the conquering of it.

MADAME MANDRAGONI.

Conquer, then!

Enter a Servant.

SERVANT.

Madam, the Prince comes this way.

BIANCA.

[*Rising, embarrassed.*

Let me go,
I pray you, kindest lady — I will wait

Here in the antechamber, till the Prince
Retires again.

[*Exit Servant.*

MADAME MANDRAGONI.

[*Showing her* FRANCESCO, *who enters.*

If the Prince gives thee leave.

[*Exit* MADAME MANDRAGONI.

PRINCE.

Stay, sweet Bianca! dost thou fly from us —
So terrible are we?

BIANCA.

[*Falling on her knees before him.*

Your pardon, Prince!
It is such bounty that confounds me quite —
Heaven's blessing be my thanks!

PRINCE.

[*Lifting her up.*

Pray on so, then!
For if that voice pierce half so deep the heavens
As it hath pierced my heart, all good will come
In answer to its call.

BIANCA.

[*Withdrawing herself from him.*

Stoop not so low
As to lift up so poor a weight as mine —
The sum of all whose value is its virtue:
For think not, Prince, that virtue I forsook,
Forsaking childhood's home.

PRINCE.

Fie, fie, Bianca!
'T is for thy virtue, more than other charms,
That thus I prize thee.

BIANCA.

Oh, then, spare it, Prince!

PRINCE.

Ay, and uplift it; giving beauty, too,
A fitter setting, where it will outshine
The jeweled favorites of emperors.

BIANCA.

I pray your Highness, let me now retire;
It is not meet that I should longer hear
Such lofty praises. I, the simple wife
Of your mean subject, all whose wealth on earth
Is my poor love.

PRINCE.

[*Retaining her hand.*

He 's richer than his prince —
I would change places with him, for that love!
But so the measure of it overfills
His largest, best capacity to hold,
That he 'll lose nothing if my empty heart
Catches the sweetness that o'erruns from his:
Thus much I 'll take, whether thou wilt, or no.

BIANCA.

All lawful love which this heart can bestow,
My Prince's right is, and my joy to give:
Permit me to take leave.

[*Courtesying, starts to go.*

PRINCE.

Stay — I 'll take mine:
But first, I have to whisper in thine ear
That soon thou 'lt change thy home.

BIANCA.

Nay, generous Prince!
Pietro's humble home now suits me well;
Love makes a palace of it.

PRINCE.

Yes; thy love
Would turn a prison to a palace: mine
Shall give that palace substance and a form.
First, I must school a too rebellious will,
To pay the penal tax of royalty,
And wed a princess with a loveless vow —
The heart meanwhile unwedded: till then, silence,
And love's adieu to thee!

[*Going.*

BIANCA.

Adieu, kind Prince!
May all work well for you, and that high lady,
Whose royal love shall bless your throne with heirs!

PRINCE.

[*Aside, going.*

Ah, royal love will never bless my heart:
Marriage may heirs bring — choice brings happiness.

[*Looking back.*

Good night, Bianca!

BIANCA.

Heaven preserve my Prince!

[*Exit* PRINCE.

So I, with power to gain a monarch's heart,
Have sold my birthright for a beggar's love!
Ah! 't is in vain to clip the eagle's wings;
For, while dispirited he stoops to mate
With farm-bred fowls below his native sphere,
His wings new-grown, from innate loftiness,
Will be replumed again erelong to soar.
I feel the stirrings of a tameless soul;
Greatness inborn asserts prerogative.
But hush, proud nature! be henceforth self-tamed;
Domesticate thee to a mean existence,
And having stooped too low to bear day's eye,
Fly to no splendor lesser than the sun's!

Reënter MADAME MANDRAGONI.

MADAME MANDRAGONI.

Forgive my rudeness, lady, since I left
Thee in good company.

BIANCA.

The hour is late,
And if it please you, Madam, I 'll retire.

MADAME MANDRAGONI.

As pleases thee.

BIANCA.

Such goodness quite confounds me.

Reënter MANDRAGONI *and* PIETRO.

MADAME MANDRAGONI.

[*To her husband.*

Wilt reconduct this gentle lady home?

[*To* BIANCA.

I would be often honored by such visits:
Forget not that my all is at your service,
And I your servant.

BIANCA.

I do blush for shame,
To be recipient of so much bounty.
Madam, I am so choked with obligation,
That thanks have no more place for utterance.

PIETRO.

And I am such a debtor to the Prince, —
As unto you, the medium of his favor, —
That gratitude is bankrupt; so, adieu!

[*To his wife, going.*

Look, here is gold!

[*Shows her a purse.*

I am first gentleman
Hence of the Prince's chamber.

BIANCA.

[*Aside.*

Is he blind?

[*Exeunt.*

MADAME MANDRAGONI.

A good beginning of an evil end!
Yet she 's so innocent, that it half smites me
To take my part in plotting 'gainst her virtue.
But we must choose 'twixt serving God and Prince;
It is not easy serving both together.

[*Exit.*

Scene V. — *The Same.*

A public square: people going and coming; some masked, some dancing, or engaged in sports, etc., celebrating the marriage of the Prince Regent *with the* Archduchess Jeanne, *of Austria. Enter two tradesmen, in masks, who stop and talk.*

1st tradesman.

Well, these are merry times for love and trade:
'T is long since Florence saw the like o' this!

2d tradesman.

Make merry while the court shines!

1st tradesman.

That I have;
And that will I; with fortune's wheel new greased
From fat of royal pleasures.

2d tradesman.

So will I!
And grease my pockets, too, 'gainst dearth of fun:
To speak the truth, they 've long been lean and lank.

1st tradesman.

Ah me! it takes all sorts to make a world.

2D TRADESMAN.

Such jackanapes as these poor fools, who dance
To their own folly, have, I do believe,
As many lives as serpents, or as cats —
Which, having nothing of them left but tail,
Will play their pranks with that.

1ST TRADESMAN.

Let us play too!
This stirring tickles even my staid shins.
Come! sing for me, and I for thee will dance.
With conscience light, the head may be light too;
We are the benefactors of this fun,
That is, we and the court; both serve one end;
The court by *giving* helps, — by *taking*, we;
That has its own share in the merriment,
And we 've our right to share it. Under mask
The court can play its tricks; so then can we,
And nothing lose of our position, either.

2D TRADESMAN.

You 'll take position, dancing — with your toes.

1ST TRADESMAN.

We, who receive all day, may give, at night,
At least a chuckle to the general laughter:
Come, haste thee, tune that windy throat of thine!

[2D TRADESMAN *sings while the other dances, and people gather round to see.*

2D TRADESMAN.

We take all day,
And give away
The night to fun and folly;
But make all pay,
Both work and play,
If sober or if jolly.

All day we cheat;
At night we meet,
And then we cheat each other;
No cheating done,
There were no fun;
All else is empty bother.

Then dance with fools!
They are the tools
We work, their purses draining!
Let mirth amuse;
They 'll faster lose,
And their loss is our gaining.

Enter a Harlequin fantastically dressed, who joins the dance.

Live, princes! live!
The gold you give,
Our pockets fast are taking;
Francesco's bride
Long live, his pride,
Each heir new fortunes making.

1ST TRADESMAN.

[*To Harlequin.*

Begone, clown! how dar'st meddle with our sport!
Hast thou no manners?

HARLEQUIN.

Manners! what are they?

1ST TRADESMAN.

I 'll teach thee, fool!

[*Kicking him.*

HARLEQUIN.

If that 's what ye call manners,
I never learned 'em, or I 'd pay you back
As mannerly as you my lesson gave —
Which I must practice on.

[*Tries to kick* 1ST TRADESMAN, *who trips him in the act, and he falls sprawling on the ground.*

1ST TRADESMAN.

You missed your lesson;
You 're a dull scholar; try again.

[*Clown jumps up, rubbing himself and laughing with the rest.*

Enter a Musician playing a dancing tune.

HARLEQUIN.

I 'll try
The dancing lesson which one of my cloth —

Who never studied manners — gave to me :
He said that I was apt at any trick,
Not a dull scholar.

1st TRADESMAN.

Then put down your foot
To prove it, and I 'll teach you manners gratis.

[*Fool dances fantastically.*

HARLEQUIN.

There, Master Manners, beat that, if you can!

1st TRADESMAN.

I 'd rather beat you!

HARLEQUIN.

Is that manners, too?

1st TRADESMAN.

Manners? You want another lesson, clown!
Then strip that tiger's skin from off your back!

[*Approaching, as to strike him.*

HARLEQUIN.

[*Defiantly, protected by the crowd.*

Hold on! blaspheme not so my festal-coat!
Know that I wear it as the favorite son
Among a good round dozen of my father;
And never honest son had better father,
As never honest father better son.

2D TRADESMAN.

[*To his fellow.*

Come, we 've played long enough the fool; away!

[*Going.*

1ST TRADESMAN.

You mean we 've long enough been played by fools.

[*Following.*

HARLEQUIN.

[*Crying after them.*

You both mean that you 've been enough befooled.

MUSICIAN.

[*Running after Tradesmen.*

Please, sirs, my pay.

1ST TRADESMAN.

Go to the devil's bank!

HARLEQUIN.

If I 'm the devil's bank, they 're mountebanks!
All other banks do give, as well as take:

[*To Musician.*

Here, man, take this, and oil thy instrument.

[*Gives him money.*

Fat faces and lean pockets go together,
And pockets fat with faces lean and lank:
For my part, I had rather fatten, giving,
Than to get lean in carrying others' fat;
And better is it to feast worms at last
Than thankless heirs, and feed the crows with bones.

[*Exeunt, all following the Harlequin.*

ACT III.

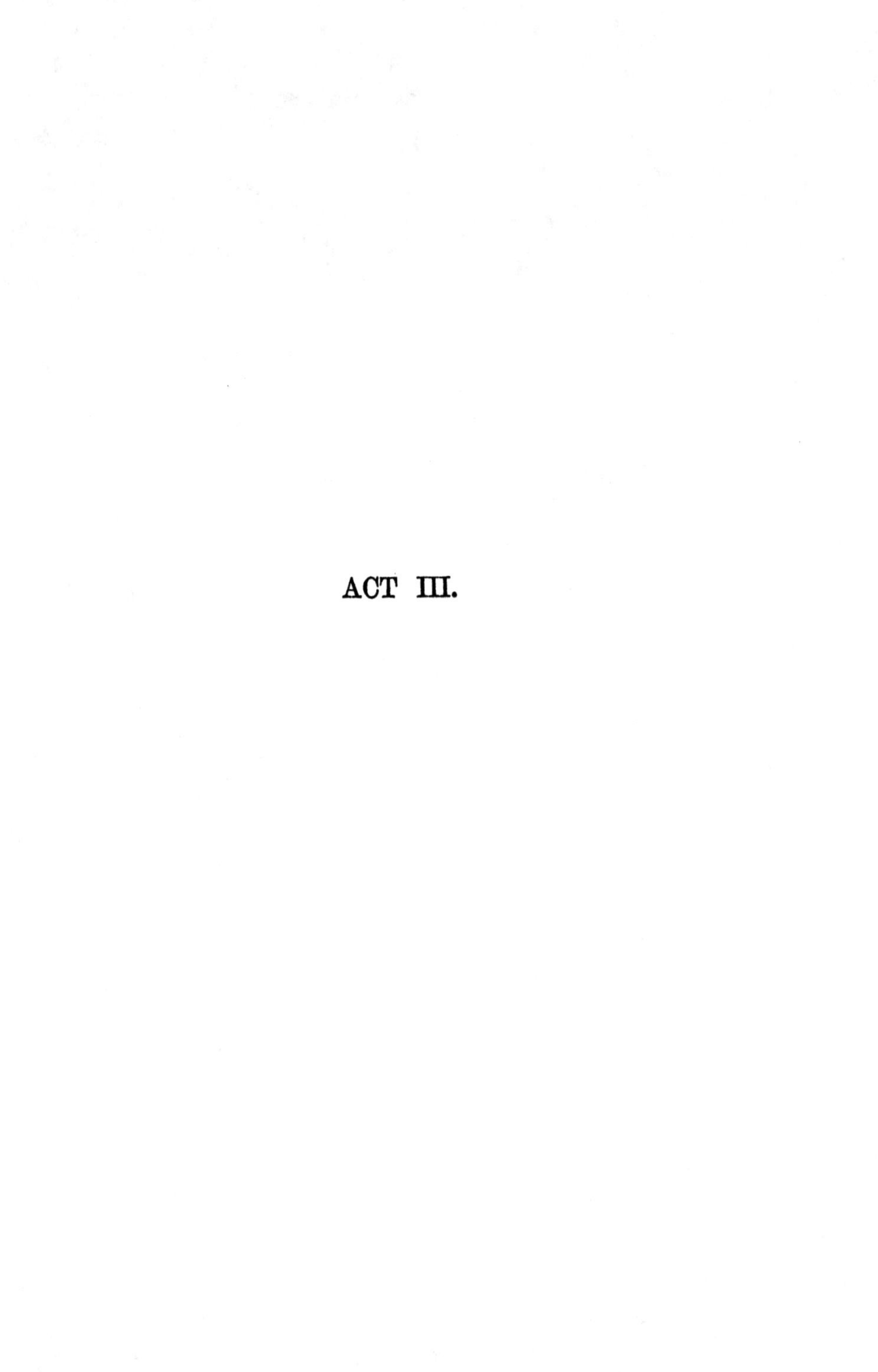

Scene I. — *The Same.*

Moonlight; garden of Bianca's *palace; in the centre a fountain with shrubbery and flowers around it; seats here and there. On one side is seen the palace, with a terrace leading from a window by steps into the garden. In front is a large gate, and in the rear a small one.* Bianca *appears on the terrace, dressed in white, looking up to the moon.*

BIANCA.

Celestial Dian! were I pure as thou,
Sleep might descend as balmily on me
As on thine own Endymion, when thy smile
Lay on him, the bright spirit of his dreams;
But now thine eye on me is set so sharply
That through the lids of mine, which fain would close,
It pierces, lancing shame into my breast.
I will descend, nor longer strive to face
Thine argent arrows, which seem ever pointed
Right at my heart.

[*Descends into the garden.*

Fresh dew, thou bath'st my feet,
As holy tears dropt on them from above;
Perhaps my angel-mother drops her tear
Among the rest — the purest gem of all.
Sweet little flowers! ye hide your modest eyes;

But I can smell the perfume of your breath —
Pure incense, rising as unspoken prayers.
And shall I breathe no prayer to blend with yours?
Perchance prayer would exorcise from my bed
The fiends Remorse and Dread, whose venomed stings
Have driven me out into the cooling night:
Yes, I will kneel beside this crystal fount,
And pray once more as I in childhood prayed.

[*Goes to kneel, when the small gate opens softly and* FRANCESCO *enters, wrapt in a mantle. She starts up alarmed, when he throws off his disguise and runs to her, supporting her in his arms.*

PRINCE.

Sweetest Bianca, fear not thus thy friend!
I only crept — as I have done each night
Since thou cam'st here — to breathe before thy gate
A prayer for blessings on thee ere I slept;
When, through still midnight, tremblingly I heard
A nightingale, whose pensive music stole
Into my heart as Love's own melody.
How could I then resist? Instinctively
This hand from out my bosom plucked a key,
And, ere I knew it, thus to me had oped
The gate of Eden, where thou art the Eve.

BIANCA.

Then be not, Prince, the serpent to beguile
My ear with flattery while my husband sleeps.
[*Withdrawing from him.*
Oh, leave me! leave me!

PRINCE.

Canst thou banish me?
Have I not long enough been exiled, then,
By austere Fate, which binds me now to one
Whom I can only honor as a wife,
While all my heart-strings tie me unto thee?
Pity thy prince, Bianca!

BIANCA.

Pity, Prince,
The frail thing, that, with favors overborne,
Bends like a reed weighed down, which strives to hold
Itself up, from pollution in the mire!
Ay, pity your Bianca!

PRINCE.

[*Seizing her hand.*

Speak again!
Oh 't was a sweet sound, *your Bianca!* Yes,
Thou art my own, and I will pity thee —
Ay, love thee, more than I do love myself;
And wouldst thou only give me in return
One drop from the rich bounty of thy love,
'T would fall as balm upon a wounded heart,
And not impoverish thine.

BIANCA.

Ah! would not mine
Be poorer then in virtue, and in peace,

For giving yours unlawfully the love
Which it hath sworn another?

PRINCE.

No! Oh no!
Believe it not! Thou didst forswear thyself
In that oath, null and void by nature's law;
Look not incensed! Nay, had Pietro's love
Been noble, it had weighed against thy birth;
But, selling thee ignobly, it hath proved
True to its parentage.

BIANCA.

Alas, 't is so!
And wherein would your love prove nobler, Prince,
Save that you are the buyer, he the seller?
And if the poor toy, now so coveted,
When gained should only weary royal hands,
Then, thrown aside with other cast-off toys,
What would its value be?

PRINCE.

Ah, wrong me not!
I swear, Bianca, by my hopeful crown,
That if we two are ever free from bonds,
I'll prove to thee that love is not caprice —
That mine is seed deep-planted in the heart,
Which will require a lifetime's growth to fill
The measure of its greatness.

BIANCA.

Cheat not, Prince,
Your royal self, nor try in vain to cheat
A woman who was never born to prove
The easy dupe even of a monarch's vow.

PRINCE.

Bianca, hear! not by yon changeful moon,
But by those steadfast stars, I swear again,
If thou wilt love me, and Heaven crowns our love
With its kind smile, through opportunity,
Thou shalt adorn, in wedlock by my side,
A ducal throne!

BIANCA.

Prince, pray, *pray* leave me now!

PRINCE.

I will obey, if, as true woman, thou
Wilt promise to obey what thy heart bids
When I am gone.

BIANCA.

Thus much I promise, Prince.

PRINCE.

While the dear vow is warm upon those lips,
Let me put love's own seal upon it — thus:

[*Kisses her.*

Now go; dews bathe in fresher bloom the flowers,

And stars grow brighter watching; starry eyes
Dim with late hours, and night airs steal from beauty
The balmy freshness of the new-blown rose:
Leave vigils to the planets; these cold damps
To the night-blooming vines; thyself to me.

[*Presses her to him; going.*

Love's choicest angels watch and keep thee safe,
Each in the apple of such eyes as languish —
Ay, in its very core!

BIANCA.

Heaven keep my Prince!

[*Exit* FRANCESCO *by the small gate.* BIANCA *stands a moment looking after him, then advances a few paces and stops.*

Who sent him here to wither on my lips
Prayer in the bud? to kill its very root
With noxious dews of an unholy love?
Am I the same I was an hour ago?
What ails me? something strange within I feel.
Who knows what this will breed? the loss of fortune
May gender fortune that will laugh to scorn
What mocked us once, and taunted our downfall.

[*Walks silently a moment, then stops with exultant air.*

To bring my lordly uncle to my feet;
To have my father kiss my hand in pride;
To see his tall, imperious wife stand back,
And wait my leave t' advance her stateliness;

I could resign all pure delights of earth —
Yea, forfeit heaven, for such a victory!
But stop, I rave! this quickening hope within
Hath made me dream impossibilities.
I had forgot, that 'twixt the thought conceived
And its full growth and birth, a barrier
Stands up, steel-clad, and strong as Death in armor.

[*Pauses a moment.*

True, once a shepherd-boy forsook his flocks,
To vanquish with a sling a giant armed,
More terrible than Death: and feeble woman
May prove too strong to shrink back from the monster.
If I gain all, and lose at last myself,
Which is to blame — my destiny, or *I*?
Fate seems to choose from out the common herd
The strongest for her own, and push them on
With a resistless force to certain ends:
Their haps and their mishaps all tend one way,
And when they seem the farthest from success,
Perchance they are the nearest: when most near,
For general good or ill, used and thrown by:
They only hang above the yawning gulf
Where Fate will hurl them to a sudden end:
Oft in her hand they are but instruments,
Themselves as nothing — what their wits work, much!

[*Walks and stops.*

I now remember, when I was a child,

An old hag, dingy as her art was black,
Who hailed me as one born to wear a crown:
These creatures are Fate's prophets, I believe,
And though the devil is himself a liar,
He makes them speak the truth: I 'll trust to this,
To princely vows, and to that regal will,
Which Nature gave me for great purposes.
High hopes! breathe into me henceforth new life:
To towering minds ye 're instinct, air, and food!

[*Exit, mounting the steps to the terrace.*

SCENE II. — *The Same.*

Street before BIANCA'S *palace. Enter two Citizens from opposite directions.*

1ST CITIZEN.

Good day, friend! what's the news?

2D CITIZEN.

Right royal news!
The Pope has crowned our Cosimo Grand Duke.

1ST CITIZEN.

That's what he went to Rome for!

2D CITIZEN.

But know you
What he's returned for?

1ST CITIZEN.

Why, perchance to take
The reins back from the Prince, and guide himself
The royal coursers.

2D CITIZEN.

Love forbid such change!

No : Cosimo best likes his titles empty ;
For him they are bell-metal, and resound
The louder, having only tongues to ring
Their glory to the kingdoms round about ;
His chief care is to have no care at all,
Save the sweet care of loving.

1ST CITIZEN.

What 's in the wind ?

2D CITIZEN.

A stately ship, with masts just newly rigged,
And gallant topsails hoisted, steering straight
For shallow water toward a harbor mean,
Where suddenly the keel is grounded fast.

1ST CITIZEN.

I 'm no interpreter of parables —
Speak plainly, man !

2D CITIZEN.

Well then, our sovereign comes
Gayly from Rome, topsailed with ducal crown,
And steers right into such a mean alliance
As marriage with his low-born mistress.[1] She
Takes two steps up : the first makes her a mother ;

[1] Camilla Martelli, second wife of Cosimo, was the granddaughter of a shoemaker. A title of nobility was given to her father, and some of his descendants are now of the noblesse of Florence.

The second, wife of the Grand Duke, forsooth,
Thus to legitimize the new-born princess.

1ST CITIZEN.

What says the Pope to that?

2D CITIZEN.

His license did it:
Our Duke, confessing to the holy father,
A pardon bought, and with it right of marriage;
So, after all, his title was not void, —
It held a wife and child.

1ST CITIZEN.

What says the Prince?

2D CITIZEN.

What say the Cardinal and the Archduchess?
The Prince has naught to say; 't is he can laugh
In secret over such a meek example
As filial love — backed by some warmer love —
One day may copy.

1ST CITIZEN.

But, the Cardinal?

2D CITIZEN.

His sacred robes can not swell big enough
To hold the fullness of his holy wrath;
Nor long enough 's the train of the Archduchess

To pin her several griefs to, with this added —
Poor royal lady!

1st citizen.

Yes: she 's poor indeed!
And Austrian pride, they say, bleeds more when hurt
Than Austrian love: we all do pity her;
Though pity 's but skin-deep, when not entwined
Round something which the heart holds: this good lady
Too cold and formal is, it seems, to suit
Our hot Italian blood.

2d citizen.

That 's not her fault;
Nor Nature's, even; but a colder climate's:
And love, you know, begets love, and can teach
The art of pleasing, more than courtly rules.

1st citizen.

Pity that this Venetian sorceress
Bewitched our Prince so, ere his luckless marriage!
See! here 's the fine cage that he keeps her in, —
Or, where she keeps him.

[*Pointing to* Bianca's *palace.*

2d citizen.

While the good Archduchess
Pines in her palace-prison all alone:
Well, well, and so, alas, the great world wags!

1ST CITIZEN.

This new-made Duchess and Bianca seem,
Through love or cunning, to be close-knit friends.

2D CITIZEN.

Not the same feather either: both fly high,
But one 's an eagle, and the other hawk.

1ST CITIZEN.

Which is the eagle?

2D CITIZEN.

The Venetian, surely:
And she will build her nest so high one day,
That mountain-winds shall tear it.

1ST CITIZEN.

But the other
Hath made already a crown-bird her prey.

2D CITIZEN.

And, hawk-like, is intent upon her prey:
The other, a true eagle, soars for power,
And preys to feed it.

1ST CITIZEN.

Why fly they together?

2D CITIZEN.

Ah, paving-stones have ears![1] we 've talked too loud,
And I, at least, too plain.

1ST CITIZEN.

Too long, you mean;
So now, adieu!

2D CITIZEN.

Give secrets iron locks!

1ST CITIZEN.

You 'll hold the keys?

2D CITIZEN.

And you your tongue. Adieu!
[*Exeunt severally.*

[1] It is said that Bianca cultivated an intimacy with Cosimo's wife, so as to get access to the Grand Duke's laboratory and learn his secret of making poisons.

SCENE III. — *The Same.*

Chamber in the royal palace. Daybreak; a light just expiring on a table covered with books and papers. CARDINAL FERDINANDO *seen alone, walking the floor impetuously.*

CARDINAL.

Sleep is for dotards! Fools and infants crawl
Lolling to Morpheus, whose soft arms I shun;
Why should the strong man, armed with his own will,
Ask patronage of a mere nursery-god?

[*The cock crows.*

Hark, there 's the cock! he is the watcher's friend,
The sluggard's foe, and sleep's dread monitor!
The sun and I together must begin
To-day our tiresome journeys.

[*Opens a door and calls* GIOVANNI.

He comes not:
Sleep hugs the hireling — as fond mothers press
Their idiot-children closest.

[*Calls again.*

Enter GIOVANNI.

GIOVANNI.

What, your Grace?

CARDINAL.

Thou sleep'st too well, boy!

GIOVANNI.

[*Rubbing his eyes.*

'T is your Grace sleeps ill:
It seems a moment only that I 've slept,
And if too well — your Grace will pardon me —
I know not what that means.

CARDINAL.

Nor can I teach
What I ne'er learned myself.

GIOVANNI.

Sleep sound is well:
To sleep too well then, must be to sleep ill;
And that your Grace can better do than I.

CARDINAL.

Thy tongue wags, boy!

GIOVANNI.

How shall I serve your Grace?

CARDINAL.

At sunrise have all ready to be off:
The horses — are they saddled?

GIOVANNI.

Yes, your Grace;
I heard hoofs clatter in the court below;
All your effects were ready ere I slept.

CARDINAL.

See if her Highness' maid, Anne, is awake,
And pray her to come here.

GIOVANNI.

I 'm sure she is.
[*Exit* GIOVANNI.

CARDINAL.

And sure am I that if the maid still sleeps,
Her mistress wakes and watches for the sun.

Enter ANNE.

ANNE.

Giovanni called me; can I serve your Grace?

CARDINAL.

I leave the city ere her Highness wakes:
Present my homage to her.

ANNE.

Would your Grace
In person render it? my lady waits
Already in her chamber.

CARDINAL.

Does she rise
At break of day? and if so, at what hour
Retires her Highness?

ANNE.

Ah, Heaven knows that best!
I left her yesternight at twelve, as bid, —
Else I had gladly waited there all night, —
And dozed as best I could, between her sighs,
Which each one pierced the thick partition wall
That separates her chamber from my own, —
Then reached and ran my poor heart through and
through.
At dawn she slowly paced the corridor;
I quickly sought her presence —

CARDINAL.

How fared she?

ANNE.

Alas! I did not ask her how she fared,
And less how she had slept; — her eyes swelled
out,
Red as hot iron, branded in my heart
The news of her ill fare.

CARDINAL.

Can I see her?

ANNE.

I'll go and ask.

[*Exit* ANNE.

CARDINAL.

Too well I knew 't was so!
The farce of power she plays makes harder still
Her powerless part behind the gilded scenes;
The crown to her will be a crown of thorns.
Fortune, who calls thee cruel is a fool!
Thou art a loon, with not enough of sense
To claim so proud an epithet as cruel;
Else why abase such inborn queenliness,
And from the way-side raise a flaunting weed
Whose odor doth offend the courtly air?
My heart scarce knows which to abhor the most,
A father's open shame, ignobly wedded, —
Or brother's half-masked infamy, which wrongs
A royal princess, pampering a minion!

Reënter ANNE.

ANNE.

Her Highness waits your Grace.

CARDINAL.

Lead on then, Anne.
[*Exeunt.*

SCENE IV. — *The Same.*

Private apartment of the ARCHDUCHESS JEANNE, *who is seen seated alone, leaning pensively on her hand; she rises and opens the casement.*

ARCHDUCHESS.

[*Looking out toward mountains seen in the distance.*

Come, morning air, fresh scented with the spring,
And fan my throbbing temples! cool these lips,
Heated and parched through feverous restlessness.
Far Apennines! I envy your blue peaks,
Which listening seem at morning's golden gate
Unto the matins of yon peaceful heaven:
When shall this soul, with earthly discords torn,
Be healed and gladdened by those harmonies?
Oh, 't is so long since gladness thrilled its chords,
That such a shock might break them!

[*Turns from the window.*

God preserve
The seed of joy maternal which I hold!
Then will this keen heart-travail, and new pangs
Its birth shall teach me, be at once forgot
In the first soul-leap of a mother's bliss.
And who can tell? my husband then may love me,
When on my bosom he shall mirrored see

The little likeness of his royal self.
I 'll pluck new heart and hope from such a chance,
And hence eat, sleep, and smile, for its dear sake:
Heaven help my tardy vow!

Enter Anne, *followed by the* Cardinal.

Good morning, Prince,
And welcome here!

CARDINAL.

How fares your Royal Highness?

ARCHDUCHESS.

Oh, better now! this morning breeze is medicine,
And cordial too: how is my royal brother?
Methinks less calm than I.

CARDINAL.

It seems so, Princess:
But I shall leave more quiet, now your face
Shows hope as victor coming on grief's track:
May I partake this joy?

ARCHDUCHESS.

No, brother, no —
You can not, unless first a woman made:
Women have anguish such as men know not;
So have we hidden springs, which yield us joy
Such as stern manhood never can partake.
But why so early, Prince?

CARDINAL.

To take my leave.

ARCHDUCHESS.

What does this mean? your Grace leaves not the court?
Does any new disaster call you hence
To other parts?

CARDINAL.

What new thing could transpire,
To equal what already plagues our court?
Madame, I cannot face a father's shame,
A brother's infamy, a princess' wrongs,
As would become a man; I must away —
I leave at once for Rome.

ARCHDUCHESS.

Take patience, Prince,
And blessings go with you!

CARDINAL.

[*Kissing her hand.*

And stay with you!

[*Exit* CARDINAL.

ANNE *shows out the* CARDINAL *and returns.*

ARCHDUCHESS.

My good Anne, know'st thou if my lord has risen?
Go ask for me his royal presence here;
And cheer up, girl!

ANNE.

My lady, I just heard
Prince Ferdinando, leaving, ask the same
Of your first gentleman.

ARCHDUCHESS.

What answered he?

ANNE.

That the Prince Regent had not yet returned
From the Cappello palace.

ARCHDUCHESS.

That 's ill news!
I would I had not heard it on this morn,
When Heaven had seemed anew to smile on me,
And I to catch that ray with gladdened heart—
Alas! as infants with their glad hands catch
At sunbeams, and then find they nothing hold!
Why didst thou tell me, girl?

ANNE.

'T was in my heart,
And so came out at my mouth's unlocked door,
As something hard to keep in: pardon, Madam!
God knows that when I so your Highness grieve,
I grieve myself more.

ARCHDUCHESS.

Yes, I know that too;

The heart from its abundance needs must speak:
Thy word was but the keen point lancing out
From a sword piercing thee: I do forgive
Its sharpness, my good Anne.

[*Gives her hand, which* ANNE *kisses.*

ANNE.

My angel-mistress!

[*Weeps.*

Woe 's me! you smile no more, except a tear
Wash out the smile as if it were a stain:
Could I but see again that smile of youth!
It haunts me like a spectre of dead joy —
Would it were yet alive!

ARCHDUCHESS.

So shalt thou see it,
The day I hear thee laugh o'er my new prince.

ANNE.

God bring such day!

ARCHDUCHESS.

Amen, good Anne, to that!

[*Exeunt.*

ACT IV.

Scene I. — *The Same.*

Royal cabinet. Prince Regent *and* Serguidi *in conversation.*

PRINCE.

Pest take the fellow! art thou sure, Serguidi,
That all these things are true?

SERGUIDI.

Ay, Prince, too sure:
The town hath long rung with his shameless vaunts:
'T is not enough for his o'erfed importance
To raise his comb and strut as cock o' the walk, —
He must keep crowing out his consequence.
I would, Prince, that his saucy neck were wrung
And he served up in broth to feed sick women;
The cause of heart-aches then would prove their cure.

PRINCE.

Such broth might suit some other maladies!
Serguidi, that sharp head of thine 's a wedge
Which straight into the knottiest questions drives,
Splitting our difficulties at a blow.
Thou hast a far sight, too; Pietro 's come

To just what thy fore-wit did say he would;
Bethink'st thee of our talk?

SERGUIDI.

Well do I, Prince:
But vanity, like every other fever,
Must have its crisis; his hath well-nigh reached it;
Life, or death, follows: death gives life sometimes,
At least new life to love.

PRINCE.

And kills love too:
This lady, whom the fellow's eyes have drawn
Into a net of discord with her father,
Might find our heart-ease broth, to her, a poison.

SERGUIDI.

Women have antidotes against such poisons:
One love 's the counter-poison of another;
Themselves die not, when dies misplaced affection;
They live to be its widows, doubly charming
For the sweet weeds of widowhood they wear,
And to place better their affections hence.
Love is a Hydra; when one head 's cut off,
Another grows; and so on, to the end.
Your Highness likes not that?

PRINCE.

We better like
Thy head, when that is longer than thine ears.

SERGUIDI.

Your Highness thinks, perhaps, I never loved.

PRINCE.

The heart loves, not the head — how could he love
Who never had a heart?

[*Walks the floor.*

SERGUIDI.

[*Aside.*

Ah, he knows not
That piqued love goads my tongue, — such heartless heads
Serve better headless hearts!

[*Aloud.*

Prince, there 's more need
Of head, than heart, at court: were princes all
Like our most gracious Regent, then the crown
Would hold itself enough of love for all.

Enter an Usher.

PRINCE.

Who is without?

USHER.

Count Ricci waits, your Highness.

PRINCE.

He need no longer wait; go bid him enter.

[*Usher brings in* RICCI, *who enters rapidly.*

What tempest hurries so your sails, my lord?

RICCI.

Your Highness will this strange disorder pardon,
And I will tell my errand.

PRINCE.

Speak out, then.

RICCI.

Pietro — bold seducer of my daughter —
Hath bolder grown, Prince, through long tolerance;
So as not only to insult her father —
Your Highness' noble and most loyal subject —
But, with implacable audacity,
Assails me in the street; and yester-night
He swore, upon a weapon at my throat,
To spill my blood if I opposed my child
In her ill-mated passion.

PRINCE.

The fiends take him!
[*Walks rapidly the room.*

SERGUIDI.

Prince, 't is the time for action, not for passion;
Your Highness will no longer see unpunished
This coxcomb vanity, grown mutinous;
Beginning thus, in its attack on nobles,
Its end will not aim lower than the crown.
[PRINCE *continues walking in silence.*

SERGUIDI.

[*Approaching* RICCI *and speaking low.*

The iron 's hot; now bend it to thy will.

RICCI.

[*Approaching the Prince.*

I pray your Highness give me leave to punish
With my own hand the assassin of my peace;
The spoiler of my house; the libeler
Of royal bounty.

PRINCE.

[*Stopping suddenly before* RICCI.

We can't give so much:
But only leave to rule and guide thyself
And thine own actions for a single day.
To-morrow to the country we retire;
And if, like Phaeton, who dared to take
The reins from Phœbus, thou dost fall thyself,
Upon thy skirts, not ours, be thine own blood:
We wash our hands here from all purple stains.

[*Goes out precipitately.*

SERGUIDI.

[*To* RICCI.

I think, together, we can guide the steeds,
Nor be ourselves the Phaetons to fall;
Brains rasher than our own must take that fate.

[*Exeunt.*

SCENE II. — *Night.*

Open space in front of a bridge crossing the Arno. A palace seen on the right, and a marble pillar near it. Enter from the bridge COUNT RICCI *and* SERGUIDI, *with one servant: they stop near the palace, looking cautiously around.*

RICCI.

[*Pointing to the palace.*

Here is my daughter's dwelling: two hours since
I saw Pietro enter; I can smell
The villain far off, as a lion scents
The thief who steals into his forest realm
For booty, and becomes himself the prey.
He 's seized his booty, now the prey is ours!
We 'll go behind this pillar.

SERGUIDI.

Hark, the clock!

[*Midnight sounds.*

RICCI.

It is the usual hour of his departing:
How oft I 've lain in wait, while heaved my breast
Like a volcano, with the wrath it held
Yet dared not vent upon the Prince's minion!

SERGUIDI.

It is the hour by which rogues keep their reckonings;
The hour that hath more vows of lovers swallowed,
Drunk in more death-sighs, and tolled out more knells,
Than all the twenty-four.

RICCI.

Take thy last kiss,
Rash youth, and welcome — we'll not grudge thee that!
Be it love's nectar, the draught deep and long.
Drink it, inebriate, even to the dregs,
And them we'll give thee! Hist! I think he comes —
Seize! — hold him fast; but leave the blow for me!

[PIETRO BUONAVENTURI *comes out of the palace; they rush upon him; a scuffle ensues, and he falls — crying out — stabbed to the heart. The murderers escape as Guards enter.*

SCENE III. — *Near Florence.*

A lawn in front of the royal villa, at Pratolino. Mountain scenery in the distance. FRANCESCO *and* BIANCA *seen walking together, the latter looking sad.*

PRINCE.

[*Stopping and taking tenderly* BIANCA'S *hand.*

Look up, Bianca — breathe this mountain air!
Why dost thou droop where everything around
Seems stirring to the kisses of the breeze,
And reveling in sweet consciousness of bliss?
This separation of our loves from court,
This sympathy with nature's fresher joy,
Makes me feel more than prince — a simple man,
With heart akin to natural delights —
Myself a loyal subject of earth's realm.
Thy pensiveness is here inopportune;
Wert thou but gayer, this to me would be
The day of all love's days the happiest.

BIANCA.

Why, Prince, so joyous? Is there nothing more
Than nature's presence which creates such change?

PRINCE.

Have I not thee, too? thou, whose coming makes
Nature exult, as a fond mother, when
Her favorite child, just sprung to womanhood,
Steps out before her decked in full-blown charms.
Earth seems to bound with joy at thy light touch;
The sky to smile serenely its content,
And every flower to tremble with delight,
In offering thee the incense of its sweets;
What want I more, when Nature joins my praise
Of her completest work?

BIANCA.

[*Looking up fondly in his face.*

There 's something more,
Which fills my Prince anew with glad content:
Now tell me all.

PRINCE.

[*Kissing her forehead.*

There is a crowning joy!
My Princess Jeanne doth promise me an heir:
But thou turn'st pale!

BIANCA.

Pale! 't is excess of joy
At your new happiness.

PRINCE.

That 's like thyself!
I only wanted thy dear smile, to put
The jewel in my crown —

BIANCA.

[*Assuming gayety.*

And wear it proudly!

Enter hastily a Court Messenger; they start forward alarmed.

PRINCE.

[*To the Messenger.*

What news on sudden brings thee from the court?

MESSENGER.

The bloodiest news, Prince!

PRINCE.

Pour it quickly, then.

MESSENGER.

[*Looking at* BIANCA.

Your Highness sees the lady well-nigh faints —

BIANCA.

[*Trying to stand, supported by* FRANCESCO.

Regard not me — obey at once thy Prince!

MESSENGER.

Your Highness' gentleman —

BIANCA.

Pietro 's dead!

[*Falls fainting into the* PRINCE'S *arms.*

PRINCE.

[*To Messenger.*

Out on thee, villain! thou hast struck a heart
Worth fifty of his lives!

MESSENGER.

[*Running for help.*

Holloa there — help!

Enter Guards and Women, who bear off BIANCA, *the* PRINCE *following.*

SCENE IV. — *Florence.*

Royal cabinet. PRINCE REGENT *sitting alone, reading a letter from the* ARCHDUCHESS JEANNE.

PRINCE.

[*Starting up excitedly, crushing the letter in his hands.*

Would she tear out my heart, then bid me live —
Take that away which stirs life's pulses, *love*,
And think to make the heart an instrument,
Beating mechanically, to keep the time
Of duty's tasks, of loveless ceremonies?
Do I not give her all a princess' right,
And more of honor, for my lack of love?
She swears she loves me; but no love is hers;
For love lives only in its object's joy,
And would die sooner than to see that marred:
Hers gives not, but demands the sacrifice —
Would banish from my sight the day itself,
And wrap me up in night to sulk with her.

[*Walks a moment and stops.*

Learn, Jeanne, that love instinctively is free,
And makes its own nest, as the forest birds
That shun with broad wing the one built for them
On garden trees, which grow perforce where planted.

Enter the ARCHDUCHESS.

[*Regarding her sternly.*

Madam, your presence honors me too much.

ARCHDUCHESS.

Would that such honor were delight instead!

PRINCE.

Suspicion is unworthy of a princess:
Bold accusation less offends the ear,
Than sly insinuation. If there lack
From me a duty, a respect, an honor,
Which from a husband to a wife belongs,
I pray you openly to name the omission,
And the debt owing shall at once be paid.

ARCHDUCHESS.

Does the heart live, then, on what duty yields?
Does it lack nothing, when all that is given
Which rigorous honor claims? The infant born
Would perish, wrapt in princeliest apparel,
Upon the softest pillow, if it lacked
The pearly fountain which its nature craved:
Love, too, may droop and die in regal state,
Unfed by that for which its being yearns;
The heart has its own food — without it, starves.

[*Kneels.*

Francesco, what I lack is love — give this!
If not for my sake, yet to feed the life

Which is a part of thine — which, thus preserved,
Shall one day give back all thou givest me.

[*The* PRINCE, *touched, tries to make her rise, but she clings weeping to his knees.*

No! no! I will die here, in asking love;
Or here receive it, and, with love, new life.

PRINCE.

[*Much moved.*

Spare me thy tears, Jeanne, and Heaven spare our child!
Is not its promise the true pledge of love?

ARCHDUCHESS.

[*Still kneeling.*

Nay: there 's a truer pledge that I would have:
Thine oath to banish her who holds the keys
Which lock me from the fountains of thy breast.
One word — oh, speak it! — swallows all my wrongs,
And floods my being with a real life!

PRINCE.

[*Lifting her up.*

I loved Bianca ere I saw thy face:
The wrong I did thee was not loving her,
But wedding thee; forgive the loveless act!
Could the heart banish, as the word can do,
Her banishment might leave thee its sole queen;
But is that banished, which, sent from our sight,
Stays ever with the unrenouncing heart?

ARCHDUCHESS.

[*Turning away weeping.*

Woe 's me, then! wherefore bring a child to light,
To join the blood of hearts, themselves unjoined?

PRINCE.

[*Aside.*

Fiends, say for me the word my lips refuse!
Love, speak it! — perjure thyself at right's altar,
And then be damned — as hence my life must be!

[*Taking hold of her.*

Stay Jeanne! stay! — on the honor of a prince —
I will — Oh, God! — yes — I *will* — banish her!

ARCHDUCHESS.

Reluctant vow! yet bless thee for it, Prince!

PRINCE.

Go, Jeanne, take peace with thee!

[*Aside.*

Leave me despair!

ARCHDUCHESS.

[*Going.*

The peace of righteous deeds remain with thee!

[*Exit* JEANNE.

PRINCE.

[*Alone, falling into a seat.*

All manhood's strength has gone forth with that vow:
I am as weak now as a vanquished purpose.
Love was my force — that oath has banished love.

SCENE V. — *Near Florence.*

Room in a convent. BIANCA *seen sitting moodily alone.*

BIANCA.

[*Rising up and coming forward.*

So fast stalks Retribution on Crime's heels?
My husband murdered — I in banishment;
Ambition struck when plumed for highest flight;
And woman's leagued powers vanquished at a blow!
Vanquished? no! no! removed to be more felt:
It is my absence that will teach the Prince
What power was in my presence. Does he think
To live without me? let him, if he can!
Poor Jeanne! she crowns her with a puppet love,
As children put on paper diadems,
And play the real, while unreal kings.
Let her play queen of my Francesco's heart,
And be as satisfied, a little hour,
As if her power were actual: all too soon
She shall behold — what she 's not made to feel —
That regal love is more supreme than law.
I can bide calmly in repose my time;
Sleep is the rest, and not the death of power.

[*Solemn music of the nuns heard without. She listens a moment.*

Cheat me not, siren tones, to gentle thoughts!
Time was when I might join that vestal hymn,
Robed in the virgin white of purity;
A crimson garment better suits me now,
And victory's note is what these lips must learn.

[*Goes to the window and looks out.*

And thou, sweet Nature! Speak not low to me
Through whispering pines, or moaning cypresses,
Or murmuring rills, or sighing nightingales;
But rather drive me to thy purposes
With goading tempests, and night-haunting owls,
Whose horrid screech but hurries daring deeds.

Enter a Nun bringing her a letter from FRANCESCO, *which she seizes triumphantly and opens. Exit Nun.*

[*Reads.*

Queen of my heart! pardon thy repentant subject. Soul of my soul! restore me thyself, and bring back life to the languishing — I die without thee! The touch of thy lips can alone absolve mine from perjury: wait not a moment — fly to this bosom, and love lend thee wings swift as my thoughts, strong as my desires, and true to thy heart's home, as to thee is thy FRANCESCO.

[*Kissing the letter, and putting it in her bosom.*

Ha! ha! already? not so soon I thought
To hear the trumpet call back to the field.
Now gathered forces march right on to conquer,

With new-gained strength new victories achieve!
'T is but to lift the crown, now at my feet,
Up to my head, and bring my foes down there.

[*Going.*

Farewell, calm sanctuary of chaste vows!
Farewell, maternal Nature! gentle tones
Of breeze, and brook, and bird, farewell! farewell!
Taunt me to action hence, defiant winds!
All elements heroic in me join;
Yet leave the veil of womanhood o'er all —
A charm to lure, a net-work to retain:
Firmness must keep what fondness first shall gain.

[*Exit.*

SCENE VI. — *Florence.*

A street. Enter two Citizens talking.

1ST CITIZEN.

[*Stopping and looking the other in the face.*

Back again! did you say — and living now at the royal palace?

2D CITIZEN.

Ay, and does that surprise you? Faith! I should be more surprised if it were not so.

1ST CITIZEN.

Was she never banished, then?

2D CITIZEN.

In sooth she was, and she was not; that is, she was banished in word and deed; but not in truth.

1ST CITIZEN.

Then she did not leave?

2D CITIZEN.

She went, without leaving: or, rather, in going, left

herself where she was; and so, came back to stay where she is.

1ST CITIZEN.

And that is, you are *sure*, in the royal palace?

2D CITIZEN.

Yes: when such as she go back one step, it is only to throw themselves forward two. She has reached the place, if not the point, she aimed at before: if found out of place, she will know how to prove herself *in* place, and make good her right and title to it. What is usurped now will be conceded anon, and the last point gained.

1ST CITIZEN.

What has she to gain more?

2D CITIZEN.

What were all she has gained, if, through it, all were not yet to be gained — or the one thing to crown all?

1ST CITIZEN.

Long live the Archduchess, to prevent that!

2D CITIZEN.

Weakness, you know, is shorter-lived than strength.

1ST CITIZEN.

Well — when Wrong puts on Lawlessness the crown,
May Right bid Liberty put License down.

[*Exeunt.*

SCENE VII. — *The Same.*

Court in front of the royal palace. A Guard standing by the grand doorway: enter, from the street, a Clown, singing.

CLOWN.

The Grand Duke dead,
Francesco's head
Now takes the ducal crown:
'T is all the same
Who 's duke, by name, —
I 'm still the royal clown.

Clowns have their tastes
When red wine wastes
At royal feasts ; — for, then,
Our wit must run,
To crown the fun
Of kings and noblemen.

We 'll mourn to-day, —
To-morrow pay
For mourning in new mirth ;
The crowning done,
There comes fresh fun
When comes a prince's birth.

[*He approaches the entrance.*

GUARD.

Have done with such untimely merriment!
Dar'st sing, wretch, while they 're saying solemn mass
In yonder church now for the Grand Duke's soul?
Hence, fool, begone!

[*Levels his weapon.*

CLOWN.

Begone thyself first! thou,
A standing armed post in this outer court,
Who dar'st assail thy better — I, who have
A standing post of honor in the court.
Fie, post! stand there against the palace door,
Whilst I shall enter in, and hold my arms
Defiant of the braggart arms you hold.

[*Runs past Guard into the palace.*

If thou wouldst have a living post, as I,
And be no more a senseless post, as thou,
I 'll tickle for thee my new sovereign's ears
With a fresh jest, and when his laugh cracks nuts,
Some kernel may have meat in it for thee:
Shall I, good guard-post?

GUARD.

Hold thy knavish tongue!

CLOWN.

If I hold that, thou still must hold thy arms!
So, when I go to air my wits in town,
Present arms next time to the royal clown —
Not at his head, for brains knock bludgeons down.

[*Exit Clown.*

SCENE VIII. — *The Same.*

Night. Dressing-room of the ARCHDUCHESS JEANNE. *On one side, leading out of it, a small oratory, with candles burning on the altar. Enter* JEANNE, *elegantly dressed, as from a ball, accompanied by* ANNE, *who carries a salver of drink, etc.*

ARCHDUCHESS.

[*Seating herself.*

Put down thy salver, Anne, and bring me now
My dressing-gown — I 'm weary of the day:
Take off these mocking jewels, which have laughed
At my poor heart, undecked by joy, too long;
And leave me then awhile — I will to prayer.

[ANNE *brings a gown and aids her to put it on.*

ANNE.

[*Taking jewels from the* ARCHDUCHESS' *hair.*

Courage, dear lady! brighter days will come.

ARCHDUCHESS.

Yes, Anne: but then my part will all be played
In this life-drama which so wearies me,
Such glittering trumpery all laid aside,
And from the scene my presence, too, retired.
But haste thee! something draws my soul to-night,

With a sweet force I can no more resist,
To the dear altar where it finds true peace;
Prayer flutters in my bosom, as a bird
That would set free its wings and soar to heaven:
Leave me a little — then return, good Anne.

[*Exit* ANNE; JEANNE *goes into her oratory and shuts the door.*

Enter BIANCA, *softly, with a phial in her hand.*

BIANCA.

It is my destiny! Why then demur?
I do what thousands have before me done,
And, doing it, crowned only their own fate.
It is the end which sanctifies the means;
I shall but send to happiness a soul
That never could be happy where it is,
And take a tiresome load of life away.
Once I had died at thought of giving death;
But outer changes change the inner nature,
Hard usage teaches to use others hard,
And living in proximity to evil
Creates a kinship between us and crime:
Guilt has become to me the friend in need,
And I obey wise counsel, doing this.

[*Goes to the salver and drops some of the liquid from the phial into the drink.*

Now good night, Jeanne; calm sleep, and be thy waking
Where thou wilt see thy hated foe no more;

There dawn thy morning brighter than on earth;
Wear thou thy crown in heaven — I'll wear it here.
[*Exit.*

Reënter ANNE, *going to the door of the oratory to listen.*

ANNE.

She prays as long as if 't were her last prayer,
And she were pouring her whole heart at once.

Reënter ARCHDUCHESS.

ARCHDUCHESS.

[*Seating herself.*

Give me now, Anne, what thou hast there for me:
I'll drink it for thy sake; though I've grown strong,
And need it not as ere I went to prayer.
[ANNE *gives her the bowl; she drinks and stops.*

There is a calm within me strangely sweet;
I do believe that I have left my woes
All at the altar; there a load has fallen
From my o'erburdened heart; it now feels light
As if it were all spirit.
[*Drains the bowl and gives it back to* ANNE.

ANNE.

And, dear lady,
I see, I *see* again in those sweet eyes
The very smile which lighted them in youth;
Oh, that is what I've longed to see once more!
Now God be thanked!

[*Aside.*

I 'm glad, and yet I weep!
There 's something in her face which touches me
More than that smile — something I never saw.

ARCHDUCHESS.

[*Rising.*

Now to my chamber with me, faithful Anne.

[*Leaning on her.*

Know'st thou, I love thee more here than at home?
There thou wast only one among my blessings;
Here my sole blessing art thou.

ANNE.

Precious mistress!

ARCHDUCHESS.

[*Walking with difficulty.*

Oh! what is this? I 'm growing strangely weak:
Hold me up, Anne, haste thee — I would to bed:
Too much I 've suffered through this tedious day —
Too much enjoyed, now, at my evening prayer.

ANNE.

Why, how you tremble! pray lean more on me;
Or let me take you in my arms, dear lady.

ARCHDUCHESS.

'T is nothing — I can walk — God bless thee, Anne!

[*Exeunt.*

ACT V.

Scene I. — *The Same.*

Royal cabinet. Francesco, *now Grand Duke, in conversation with* Serguidi.

FRANCESCO.

My conscience owes it, and my ghostly father
Wills it of me, as but to virtue due;
And since my heart jumps with the will of Heaven,
It shall at once be done.

SERGUIDI.

'T is well resolved —
A Christian act, one worthy of a saint.
Conscience and justice could alone demand
To sanction love's vows with the Church's blessing;
And this your Royal Highness promptly did
When the Archduchess Jeanne was snatched from earth.
A public recognition of those rights
Due to a sovereign's wife, and long-tried love,
Puts on your ducal head a double crown,
Lifts a high spirit to its natural seat,
And brings proud Venice to the feet of Florence.

FRANCESCO.

Command a noble envoy to be sent
Without delay from hence to the Republic,
Announcing in right royal pomp our will,
And naming the glad day of coronation,
Whose splendor shall make bright the realms around.
Let heralds, too, be sent to other parts,
Proclaiming it as far and wide as spreads
The fame already of the Medici;
And send a special messenger to Rome,
To bid Prince Ferdinando to the feasts;
While we take on us the most pleasant part,
And break the welcome tidings to our spouse.
[*Going.*

SERGUIDI.

All shall be done with cheerfulest dispatch.
[*Exit* Francesco.

Was ever wanton's triumph more complete?
So, *will* is power — the battle to the strong!
Well, martyrs go to heaven through fire and blood;
And she, as well, has gained her heaven — the throne.
Poor dotard sovereign! then thou knewest not
That 't was Bianca — feigning goodness' voice —
Who spake to thee through perjured priestly lips?
Her crown should have a bloody ruby set
Amid its gems, the largest one of all,
To blush forever for its wearer's guilt,
And tell the world it was the price of blood.

None will suspect how dearly it was bought,
Save I, alone; and crime, to me, becomes
Virtue, when based upon so grand a scale.
Prince Ferdinando 't is who will rebel;
Ah, ha, Francesco! think'st thou he will grace
This coronation? no! he 's cardinal,
And hath not made his labyrinthine way
Through priesthood's coils, to be entrapped by woman.
Woe to her and her crown, if he does come,
And deadlier woe, if, coming, he should smile!
The wiliest poisoner may out-poisoned be —
A match for any Medicis is she!

[*Exit.*

SCENE II. — *The Same.*

Throne room. Flourish. Enter FRANCESCO *and* BIANCA, *in ducal robes and crowned, preceded by guards, and followed by officers and ladies in waiting, courtiers, etc. The ducal pair take their seats on the throne, and the lords and ladies their several positions.* SERGUIDI *seen on the right of the* GRAND DUKE.

FRANCESCO.

[*To an Usher.*

Bid enter now the embassy from Venice.

[*Usher leads in a brilliant cortege headed by* PATRIARCH D'AQUILEA *and* BARTOLOMEO CAPPELLO, *with his wife and her son* VITTORIO.

Seigniors! right noble senators! and all
Who from the great Republic, greeting, come,
We bid you welcome to our own domain!
With special honor to th' illustrious kin
Of her who shares our confidence and crown.

AQUILEA.

[*Coming forward.*

All hail, majestic sovereign! hail, fair bride! —
The proudest scion of a lordly house —
To us allied by fondest ties of blood.

[*Kneels.*

Your Highnesses we greet here, in behalf

Of grateful Venice — kneeling at your feet;
And cordial salutations from her Doge
Bring, with this gem of true imperial wealth,

[*Presents a magnificent diamond to* BIANCA.

A bridal gift, befitting her proclaimed
Especial daughter of the great Republic,
For those rare gifts — but equaled by her virtues —
Which have gained for her proofs of highest favor,
And sealed her right to share a ducal crown.

BIANCA.

[*Motioning him to rise.*

I do accept the proud gift of the Doge,
And all your homage, friends, with liberal thanks.

[FRANCESCO *and* BIANCA *descend from the throne.*

BIANCA.

[*To her father.*

Since Fortune hath to blessing turned thy curse,
Which once fell on me as a withering blight,
Revoke it, through paternal benediction,
Without which, diademed, I 'm still uncrowned.

CAPPELLO.

Poor now, my daughter, is thy father's blessing!
But, turned to prayer, it may secure thy crown
Heaven's richer benediction in its stead;
Be that thy glory, and thine heritage!

[*Kisses her hand.*

BIANCA.

[*To her step-mother.*

Come forward, noble lady, and behold
The salutation which we give thy son,
Who called us *sister*, when thou saidst not *daughter*;
And whom, as then, we proudly here now call
Brother — *we*, daughter now of the Republic!

[*Embraces* VITTORIO; *gives her hand to her uncle; courtesies coldly to* LADY CAPPELLO, *who abases her head, and retires, led by* FRANCESCO, *and followed by the retinue. Flourish.*

SERGUIDI.

[*Alone.*

Out of the same lips cursing comes, and blessing!
Have crowns such might then, as turn maledictions
To benedictions and paternal prayers?
Thus Innocence, once cursed for having fallen
Below its parentage, in lawful love,
When changed to baseness may in turn be blest,
If it, in changing, rise above its birth
And chance to legalize unlawful love.
Oh, what a great transformer is Position!
It makes that, which, being low, was foul and hideous,
Turn pure and beautiful in rising up:
So, henceforth, damned be Virtue, if low placed,
And blest be Crime, if raised to wear a crown.

[*Exit.*

SCENE III. — *The Same.*

A library. CARDINAL FERDINANDO *in conversation with* FRA FORTUNATO. SERGUIDI *enters unperceived, and conceals himself behind them.*

CARDINAL.

The evil has become a foul excrescence
Upon the glory of the crown and state.

FRA FORTUNATO.

There is no cure for evils such as these,
And their removal can alone restore
Health to the state: our body politic
Needs now a skillful surgeon.

CARDINAL.

Where to find one
Is, then, the question we must here decide.

[*Pauses.*

SERGUIDI.

[*Aside.*

Here priesthood is a monster with two heads,
And, as I thought, complotting treachery!
But I'll be privy to it, and compel

His Eminence to make me, erst his foe,
His friend henceforth, through fear, if not through love;
Ay, minion, because holder of his secret.
[*Listens again.*

FRA FORTUNATO.

Your Grace knows well that painful operations,
On which depend alone the general good,
Are never cruel; nor the hand which works them
Other than that of a wise benefactor;
Service to state is service done to Heaven.

CARDINAL.

Then who so fit as Heaven's own ministers
To do such service?

FRA FORTUNATO.

None, your Eminence!
And when Heaven's sanction strengthens princely right,
That which to others would be even crime,
Becomes, for righteous ends, the highest virtue.

CARDINAL.

But there are deeds that Righteousness approves,
Which common laws unrighteously condemn;
For human justice is conventional.

FRA FORTUNATO.

True : so, such deeds must be in secret done.

CARDINAL.

What 's done in secret then must be well done,
And wisest heads need coadjutors too.

FRA FORTUNATO.

Your Eminence has only to command.

CARDINAL.

Then, listen ! our state-evil is this woman ;
Her power the excrescence which must be cut off;
We are the surgeons ; the Church our diploma ;
God's grace our fee ; our end, to work a cure.

FRA FORTUNATO.

If my poor services — whose chief of merit
Is in devotion to the cause of right —
Can aid this cure, your Eminence will use them.

CARDINAL.

I mean to lie in wait : behold this ring !
'T will test the subtlest poison, turning pale
Through contact, as a jealous wife brought near
The rival aiming to seduce her spouse :
I will not eat nor drink till I apply
To all before me, first, this conscious stone ;
When its changed color signals *treachery*

I 'll turn the serpent's sting back on herself,
And thus may free my own skirts from her blood:
But, if blood must be spilt, to cleanse the state,
And to atone for crimes in her high places,
Our priestly office suits such sacrifice:
Be ready then — just acts meet just rewards.

FRA FORTUNATO.

My humble efforts have their recompense
Serving your Grace, and so the general weal.
[*Starts back, seeing* SERGUIDI, *who discovers himself.*

CARDINAL.

[*To* SERGUIDI.

What dost thou here? how have thy daring steps
The threshold crossed of sacred privacy?

SERGUIDI.

It matters little when, or how, I came,
If but my visit hath the honest end
To serve your Eminence; for doing which,
I needed first to understand your plans.

CARDINAL.

Knave! thou wert sent here as the spy of power,
To which thy craftiness is but too loyal!

SERGUIDI.

Suspicion, I protest, deceives itself:
But say it rightly speaks; 't were wise to make

A friend perforce of evil luck, and turn
That to advantage which might work against us:
I hold your secret; — by consent, or no,
Boots not, if he who holds hath will to keep
And mind to serve it.

FRA FORTUNATO.

[*Regarding* SERGUIDI *obsequiously.*

If I dared advise
Your Eminence, I should in justice say
That he, who hath served long and faithfully
One prince's will, may serve as well another.

CARDINAL.

Serguidi, to change masters argues change
Of purpose, too: yet, mark — if in appearance
Thou dost change only, worse the end for thee!
But if thou wilt change truly, and dost prove
As apt a servant on the side of truth,
As thou hast proved before on falsehood's side,
Right, when in power, shall make thee its fast friend.

SERGUIDI.

What now your Eminence is forced to do
May be re-done a later day, by choice.

CARDINAL.

[*Going out, to* SERGUIDI.

Await here, thou, until I come again.

[*To the Monk.*

Adieu! till thou shalt learn my farther will.

[*Exit* CARDINAL.

FRA FORTUNATO.

[*To* SERGUIDI.

Here is my hand — 't is given in honest faith.

SERGUIDI.

[*Sarcastically, taking his hand.*

And taken in a faith no less sincere.

FRA FORTUNATO.

[*Aside, going.*

Make league with devils, when you 're in their
power.

[*Exit.*

SERGUIDI.

Oh, what a mockery is this religion!
What lying hypocrites its ministers!
There goes a wolf so hungry after gain
That he can lap up blood which others spill;
And yet he wears sheep's clothing: so does he
Who hath employed him, princely Ferdinand!
But the wolf 's in his face; while this false monk
Puts on the sheep's look too, and through it serves
Better the ends for which he is engaged.
Bad masters must have servants bad as they,
Only dressed up in liveries of truth;
As Satan must have aids, and can't employ

Angels for ministers ; so he takes fiends.
On fiendish errands angels would be fools,
Making lies visible in candor's light ;
While a fiend, borrowing an angel's face,
Keeps his lies hidden underneath the mask.
Thank Heaven ! I wear no Church's livery —
The court's suits well enough my purposes ;
And this I must maintain for future ends,
Even at the sacrifice of ancient friends.

Scene IV. — *Near Florence.*

Night. Chamber in the royal villa, Poggio à Cajano. Enter Giovanni *with a salver of wine, etc., which he sets on a table and goes out. Enter, soon after,* Bianca.

BIANCA.

[*Looking about her carefully.*

I left him hard at play, and bent on winning;
So he will not disturb my own by-play:
He has dismissed his valet for the night,
And none will here be scenting out my game.
Now, Vengeance, come — thou sweet, as terrible!
Come execute the sentence, long delayed,
Of pitiless justice on this devil's spy!
Once 't was ambition turned to steel the nerves
Which laced my woman's nature; then I rose
On murdered Innocence, my stepping-stone:
Now, mounted to the apex of desire,
I 've naught to gain; 't is but to keep the seat
Whence I hurl vengeance on a climbing foe.

[*Drops poison into the wine.*

Now, Cardinal, play on! win one more game —
It is thy last: our lingering game I 've won.

[*Exit.*

Enter FRANCESCO *and* FERDINANDO *together.*

CARDINAL.

Brother, your sovereignty was pressed to-night;
But you are used to losing.

FRANCESCO.

You to gaining!
Now, tell me, did you ever lose a game?

CARDINAL.

Not since I lost a boy's smooth upper lip:
But you are piqued! come, drown the grudge in wine.

[*Pours out two cups of wine, gives one to the* GRAND DUKE, *and applies his test ring to the other. Retakes the cup from* FRANCESCO.

Stay! drink it not! Revenge hath passed this way,
Breathed on our wine, and turned it into poison!

FRANCESCO.

What is there in thy dark insinuation?
Uncover its black heart; or, on the point
Of justice' lance I'll pluck it, piece by piece!

CARDINAL.

Nay, brother, be not angered! 't is thy wife
Whose heart is black with vengeance, and hath mixed
Its venomous blood with this red wine, for me.

FRANCESCO.

Dost hurl lies at us? in our proper face
Dar'st thrust thy malice? give me back the wine —
I 'll drink it, and thus prove thee false as hell!

CARDINAL.

Nay, do it not!

FRANCESCO.

Give me the wine, I say!

[*Seizes the cup.*

CARDINAL.

Drink it, then! at the peril of your throne,
Your life, your soul, and your wife's damned spirit!

[FRANCESCO *drinks.*

BIANCA.

[*Rushing wildly in.*

Throw down that cup, as thou dost love thy life!

[*Dashes the cup from his lips.*

FRANCESCO.

If death was in the cup, then I am dead —
For I have drunk it!

BIANCA.

Oh, avenging Heaven!
Most cruel when most just! the wine was poisoned,
To save thy life and punish a vile traitor.

CARDINAL.

[*To* BIANCA.

Then drink it, and be punished!

FRANCESCO.

Rebel, hold!
We will not see our Princess outraged thus
By wrath grown bold in hope of power — begone!

[*Exit* CARDINAL.

BIANCA.

[*Throwing herself into her husband's arms.*

Oh, God! I did it — I, who loved thee so!

FRANCESCO.

'T was Fate who did it — accuse not thyself!

[*Growing ill.*

But what is this I feel — can it be death?
No, 't is not death — it is my heart-strings tearing!
Life's ties may all be severed, throne and state
Rent from me, yet give no such mortal pang
As this — this violent parting of our loves!

BIANCA.

Alas! alas! and he has loved me thus!

FRANCESCO.

Kiss me, Bianca.

[*She kisses him.*

Oh, that kiss runs through

Life's shattered chords, as heaven's electric shock
Through the torn fibres of a tree uprooted!
Kiss me again, it mocks me with new life,
Dead thing as now I am! But must we part?

BIANCA.

Woe stays with me — thou goest to meet thy joy.

FRANCESCO.

Is there existence, then, where thou art not?
No! no! for me there is no life to come;
Thou art my life — I leave my heaven in thee.

[BIANCA *goes from him and pours out some of the wine.*

BIANCA.

[*Holding up the cup.*

Our loves shall not part — see, Francesco, see!
I drink where thou hast drunk — I die with thee.

FRANCESCO.

[*Trying to reach her, but falling in the attempt.*

Drink not; my love shall never kill thee — live!

[BIANCA *drinks.*

Oh, God, she drinks! now heart and soul hug close:
Ye shall not be asunder torn — fear not!

[*She drains the cup and runs to her husband, supporting his head on her bosom.*

BIANCA.

'T is done! now sleep thy last sleep on this breast,
Which hath long pillowed, love, thy fondest dreams.

O Heaven! I ask no mercy for myself —
I have to others been unmerciful —
But let this true, sweet spirit pass aneled
From every contact foul with mine, blood-stained:
Mercy, forgiveness, peace, kind Heaven, for him!

FRANCESCO.

Grant me no mercy, Heaven, which she shares not:
Else pardon to my spirit were not peace;
Nor mercy aught, save most unmerciful.
If any stain of sin be found on her,
That stain I own — its punishment be mine;
Or, pardoning that, save both souls from its curse!

BIANCA.

Amen! alas, 't is all crime dares to say!

FRANCESCO.

My lips grow icy — warm them with thy breath —
The gales of paradise are not so sweet!
Oh, joy! for *love* there is a life to come;
There we shall grow, in loving, young again,
There will I give thee an unfading crown:
Cling closer! do not let me go alone.
Come — I am going — one more kiss — one more —
[*Dies.*

BIANCA.

[*Growing ill and rising with difficulty.*

We, who have slept on softest beds, spread o'er

With royal purple, must die here as dogs
Upon the floor, uncared for and unwept.
'T is fearful, meeting death thus all alone!

[*Looks about terrified, going towards the corpse, but falls suddenly on her knees, fancying she sees the* ARCHDUCHESS JEANNE.

What see I there? O Jeanne! O spirit good!
If greatness be forgiving, pray for me;
If gladness can to woe be pitiful,
Pity me, for remorse is pitiless!
I did not hate thee; frown not so on me —
I took thy life but to enrich my own.

[*Fancies the vision points to her husband.*

Nay, look not thus! I did not mean to kill him,
Yet now I die atoning for the act.
Turn off that eye — it sinks into my heart
As cold and heavy as a leaden weight —

[*The vision fades.*

O fiends, torment me not before the time!

[*Clasps her hands in agony, again seeing the vision.*

Smile once on me — forgive, pure shade, forgive!
If angels pardon, God may pardon too.

Enter CARDINAL FERDINANDO, *with* SERGUIDI *and* FRA FORTUNATO.

CARDINAL.

[*Observing his dead brother.*

Justice is working — let us to its aid!
Dead monarch, thou no subject hadst so true

As thou thyself wast servant unto love;
Cold recompense is death for such warm serving.

[*To* BIANCA, *who continues kneeling by the body.*

What! on thy knees, at last! those prayers are vain;
Blood ne'er was spilt that had such cleansing power
As to wash princes' blood from thy stained soul;
Cease praying then, and turn thee unto dying,
For thou must drink the cup prepared for me.

[*Pours out wine and offers it to her.*

BIANCA.

'T is drunk already: thou hast lost thy victim.
Turn hate then into mercy, and forgive!

CARDINAL.

Crime's Gorgon head hath turned my heart to stone,
Nor could compassion's subtlest alchemy
Change into mercy hatred hard as mine.

BIANCA.

Then pardon Heaven! as I die pardoning thee.

[*Falls on the body of* FRANCESCO *and dies.*

CARDINAL.

Justice be thanked, I am no murderer!

FRA FORTUNATO.

Hell opens to receive her soul unshriven!

CARDINAL.

Stand ye as witnesses that her own will
Herself hath punished; that her dark intent —
Hurled back — fell, blasting as the bolt of vengeance,
Heaven-aimed, upon the fortress of her power.

FRA FORTUNATO.

So perish every enemy of God!

SERGUIDI.

So perish every foe of Ferdinand!

CARDINAL.

[*To* SERGUIDI.

Give thou the charnel-house her dainty body,
To serve, with felons' flesh, at wormy revels:
She thought, in dying with her monarch-lover,
To lie still with him in a royal tomb —
Lodged in the chapel of the Medici.
No! let Francesco sleep there with his spouse,
While this, his mistress, rots with courtesans.

[*To* FRA FORTUNATO.

Come thou with me — we must alarm the house,
And double confirmation asks such deeds.

[*Exeunt* CARDINAL *and* FRA FORTUNATO.

THE END.

www.ingramcontent.com/pod-product-compliance
Lightning Source LLC
LaVergne TN
LVHW021410110826
845150LV00007B/1868

* 9 7 8 1 4 2 5 5 1 1 2 2 7 *